SURVIVING
MAMA

SURVIVING MAMA

Overcoming Strained Mother-Daughter Relationships

An Adult Daughter's Guide

Dr. Pamela Everett Thompson

For information about this title or to order other books and/or electronic media, contact the publisher:
Building Bridges to Better Lives
950 Dannon View, St. 4201, Atlanta, GA 30331
www.survivingmama.com or www.drpamthompson.com

ISBN: 978-0-9831889-0-2

Printed in the United States of America

Cover and Interior design: 1106 Design

Dedication

This book is dedicated to my heavenly Father, the inspiration for this book and my entire life. All glory and honor is due to Him.

I also dedicate this book to my mother, Dorothy Everett, affectionately known to me as "Charlie." I thank her for being my biggest cheerleader, for always demonstrating gladness whenever she sees my face, and for always being open to hearing my concerns. I will not forsake her many life lessons imparted to me in words and deeds.

Acknowledgments

I AM DEEPLY GRATEFUL TO THE subjects of this book, who shared their struggles with such impressive willingness and a desire to be helpful to future readers who may have similar challenges. They richly blessed me with their trust and their stories, and I am privileged to know their secrets.

I want to thank my husband, Ezra, for the time sacrificed while I spent countless hours writing, reading and editing this book. His colorful use of metaphors from his mid-western roots helped me paint more vivid pictures for the readers whenever I felt stuck. I am enormously grateful to my writing coach, Ellie Wharton, who helped me to transform my clinical writing style into what I hope is enjoyable reading. She held me accountable to completion of this work well above and beyond the call of duty. I relied heavily upon her honest and refreshing feedback. I am indebted to Stephanie McIver and Dr. Nathaniel Griffin, who eagerly devoted time and careful attention to reading my first completed draft. They offered the initial feedback that allowed for a cleaner editing process by the kind and supportive professionals at 1106 Design. I also have to acknowledge several others who poured over possible titles and book cover designs and/or provided encouragement in general. They include Javonne Hines, Dr. Cheryl Williams, Tjames Scott Macauley and Mary Macauley, Kelly Seltzer, and Dr. Rachael Elahee.

Table of Contents

I Love My Mother,
But I Don't Like Her

MOTHER. MOM. MAMA. MADEAH. THESE terms of endearment conjure up portraits of matchless tenderness, caring and love. Just think of how the Spinners pulled at the heart strings with their soul-stirring, tear-jerking 1975 rendition of the memorialized "Sadie" with lyrics like, "she's teaching angels how to love." Mama, it seems, might just trump Jesus in some cultures. Or watch any televised sporting event and you'll see massively built athletes mouth "Hi Mom!" under the glare of television cameras, yearning to make her proud (rarely, if ever, have I seen Dad get a shout-out). Or recall pompous politicians transformed into humble servants as they gingerly extend manicured hands to usher Madeah onto the stage. They understand that caring for *her* outweighs the demands of the audience and they better not EVER forget it.

Greeting card companies stake second quarter profits on the sale of eloquently rhyming sentiments on Mother's Day. For many it is a day that provokes pilgrimages from near and far. These sojourners are compelled to pay homage to Mother on that day and join her for perhaps their only trip to church that year. So who would ever think that in the hushed silence of a therapist's office or within the deepest places of a confidential relationship, someone dares to boldly admit the unthinkable: "I...well...uh...uh...ur...don't like my mother."

Whether this sentiment is stated bluntly or expressed in so many ways, this "confession" requires the most trusting of relationships to be explored fully. I always admire the courage it takes for these brave souls to evolve from timid expressions of their honest feelings to liberating convictions. When perceiving Mama as a saint among saints is culturally sanctioned, no matter how dysfunctional she may be, dismantling her pedestal may seem as insurmountable a task as David's battle against Goliath.

How does one arrive at this place of disliking the woman who served as the earthly vessel that made life possible? The reasons run the gamut. At one extreme, those reasons may include a neglectful mother who allowed her daughter to be sexually or physically violated by her significant other or who may have served as the perpetrator of abuse herself. At the opposite extreme, the reasons may spring from a doting mother who, alongside her chicken and dumplings, served up dishes of control or guilt until the parent-child relationship was reduced to one of mere obligation or appeasement. One factor that allows toxicity in the relationship to fester is close-minded mothers who resist or deflect constructive feedback regarding their parental influence. The maturity required for open-mindedness and non-defensiveness about the job one did as a parent is a rare jewel. Emotional maturity, regardless of chronological age, encompasses insight—the ability to step outside of oneself and see one's own flaws and foibles with some degree of objectivity and ownership of one's impact on others *without* excuse. To embrace the whole kit and caboodle of who one is (good, bad and ugly) is the mark of the type of maturity that has the potential to save the most broken of relationships, including deeply scarred parent-child kinships. Most arguments, conflicts or feuds can be easily averted if one party is simply willing to *acknowledge* wrongdoing and demonstrate interest in considering a matter from another's perspective, even when there is disagreement on those perspectives. A simple but heartfelt "my bad" would speak volumes and go a long way toward opening dialogue and making inroads on building a genuine and intimate relationship.

There is one quick litmus test that determines the absence of emotional maturity in the mother and provides valuable information to the daughter about how to proceed in relationship with Mama. This test renders its ugly results when an adult daughter reflects upon hurtful or downright degrading experiences with her mother. She decides to give voice to them in what she hopes will be a "Hallmark Moment." When she makes the brave decision to empty her soul to Mama in a desperate search for healing and reconciliation, acknowledgment and even apology, she may be met instead with a jolt of reality. Mama may respond curtly, "Well I did the best I could...I'm sorry if you got your little feelings hurt...I worked my butt off for you, and you ought to be grateful...you had more than I could have ever imagined...I don't know where you got all these ideas about what I supposedly did to you...I do not know what you're talking about." This dismissive and debasing verbiage is poisonous. However, it is *useful* in helping the daughter understand how ill-equipped her mother is for mature relationship at that given time. Unfortunately, the relationship may never recover from such an inconsiderate response. Only the most determined and forgiving of daughters will venture back into such a cauldron that is boiling over with distasteful or even bitter reflections. In Mama's mind, she has apparently rewritten the story of her daughter's childhood and has decided to re-canonize herself as the saint she always thought herself to be. Nevertheless, there is still hope for this relationship to thrive in some capacity if the daughter desires to push through her pain and persevere toward peaceful acceptance. Once the daughter learns how to clothe herself in a fireproof apron, she can indeed stand the heat in the kitchen with Mama and learn how to navigate an adult relationship with her. She will recognize and guard against the ingredients in the relationship that are too acidic to digest and learn to savor the flavors that give the relationship its robust endurance.

This book will contain material from psychological literature coupled with biblical parallels and instruction with universal themes that may also apply to father-son, father-daughter and mother-son relationships in all ethnic groupings. However, the work originates from stories of mother-daughter relationships primarily in the African American community. In my observations, certain socio-cultural-historical factors exist among African Americans that make the already complex mother-daughter relationship more challenging to navigate. It is a relationship that is perhaps more interdependent and intensely protected throughout the daughter's lifespan than in other ethnic groupings. Additionally, I'm interested in exploring this subject from an African American perspective because the stereotypes of groupthink in this culture are sometimes true in that there may be tremendous peer pressure to move and think as one unit. Hence, differentiation from the code of conduct expected by one's parents, family, friends or culture carries with it the risk of nullifying one's "Black card," which may create unwanted and undeserved isolation. Generally speaking, thoughts and actions that are independent of cultural norms may not be celebrated or encouraged in minority communities. As a result, African Americans vote overwhelmingly for one political party and may mock those who go against the grain of culturally dictated food choices, recreational choices, relationship choices or certain church traditions. Hence, a daughter weighed down by conflicts with her mother in an African American context may consider it too taboo to disclose her honest feelings about her "saintly" mother and may choose to suffer in silence. She may not allow herself to even consider that empowering alternatives for negotiating that relationship are indeed available to her.

As a psychologist, I am passionately interested in all sorts of relationships. I never cease to be amazed at how some individuals continue to play a certain role with family and friends against better judgment, simply because that's the way it's always been done or because of bondage to what people will say or think. Consequently, resentment, frustration and feelings of inadequacy build while people "suck it up" and fall in line with the expectations. I see this often in individuals' relationships with their mothers. I will share some of these stories—all of them true—throughout this book.

From the experiences of my private practice and my work in a women's prison, I am acutely aware that some women would rather endure eating disorders (including plain old overeating), self-injury (e.g., cutting themselves), incarceration, forfeited dreams, unused talents, drained finances, unhealthy influences on their children or imploding marriages rather than call Mama out on her foolishness (as we say in the South) without guilt or second-guessing. I wrote this book because it is my calling to highlight the intersection of clinical and biblical perspectives as they pertain to concerns, challenges and practical problem-solving in everyday relationships. In so doing, I aim to encourage those who suppress their suffering in relationships in favor of a happy façade and a pseudo-existence. Authentic living empowers a person to seek liberation, healing, renewal of mind and purpose and righteous direction for the future. It is my hope that this book will promote self-awareness, forgiveness, reconciliation and assertiveness for women to peacefully live the life God planned for them long before they were in their mothers' womb. "There is surely a future hope for you and your hope will not be cut off" (Proverbs 23:18).

CHAPTER ONE

The Sins of the Mother
Are Visited Upon the Child

LITA IS JUST EIGHT YEARS OLD and even at this young age she is caught between a rock and a hard place. Her parents never married and have not lived together since she was five. At first glance anyone can see that her father, Devon, has "issues." He never finished high school and makes little money working as a sometimes painter, sometimes sheet-rocker and sometimes yard worker. Nevertheless, he delights in providing for his little girl and makes her needs a top priority. In fact, Lita is Devon's *only* reason for persevering in his efforts to get on his feet in a city where he attracts bad luck like sugar attracts ants. With deceased parents, no siblings in town and no genuine friends to speak of, Devon's life is one of loneliness so burdensome that anyone who engages in conversation with him immediately feels the anvil-like weight of his isolated existence and the toll it takes on him. However his life has one bright spot so blinding that it is impossible to overlook—Lita. His wearied face never fails to sparkle with unspeakable joy when Lita is in sight.

One Christmas, Lita put her two nickels together to buy him a thick, soft pair of socks for work. Devon visibly choked up and was hard-pressed to speak even one word. He beamed with pride and welled up with such tearful emotion that he could have been confused with a father about to escort his daughter down the aisle on her wedding day.

Lita loves Devon and knows that he adores her. Yet, at the same time Lita feels a strong loyalty to her mother, Cynthia, even though Cynthia has not always been loyal to her. Cynthia had in fact abandoned Lita when she was five, leaving her in the care of Devon for a year when she moved to another state to kindle a new love with whom she had been corresponding by phone. Even before she left, Cynthia had hardly participated in Lita's life outside of food and shelter. She missed Lita's pre-K graduation and rarely, if ever, came to see her perform at church. Lita went to church by herself, even as a five-year-old, often catching a ride on the church van while her mother slept. The same Christmas that Devon was bowled over by Lita's gift of socks, Cynthia responded with utter indifference at Lita's gift of colorful, fragrant candles, selected with much care. Cynthia glanced at the gift with less interest than one displays when presented with a stack of bills.

Nevertheless, Lita longed for Cynthia during that year of absence. Once, while silently suffering in church, she erupted in tears, drawing attention to herself from several concerned congregants as she was walked out in a fit of uncontrollable sobbing. She couldn't find the words to describe why she was crying or tie her reaction to anything that precipitated it. After minutes passed, Lita mustered up the words: "I just want to see my mom."

When her mother finally returned with her new husband, Lita was "oh so open" to picking up where she and Cynthia had left off, even wanting to skip school to be with her mother. She accepted the new stepfather, Olson, despite her confusion over Cynthia's instructions that Devon was no longer her father. Overnight, Olson had become "daddy." Lita complied with the new family order even as Devon persevered in maintaining his relationship with her by visiting often and keeping up with her whereabouts and needs.

At this writing Lita is eight, and it is getting harder for her to understand Cynthia's perplexing ways, which often put her at odds with her feelings toward Devon. Additionally, Cynthia often instructs Lita to lie for her about any number of things— silly things where the lies make no difference to any particular outcome. As a younger child, Lita was oblivious to Cynthia's moral shortcomings. Now, Lita is feeling *major* conflict over the lies. For example, when they recently moved to a new location, Cynthia instructed Lita to tell Devon that she doesn't know where they live. This prevents Devon from picking Lita up for fun Sunday afternoons spent at the park or McDonald's for a quick bite. Lita hates lying, which goes against everything she is taught at school and church, but how can she be disobedient to her mother? Isn't that also wrong? And yet, how can she be dishonest with her father who has never abandoned her? It is a lot for an eight-year-old brain to process.

Psychology calls Lita's dilemma a double-bind, one heck of a quandary where equally important values and demands oppose each other against one's will or are out of one's control with harmful consequences in either direction. In other words, the child is damned if she does and damned if she doesn't.

It will likely be a couple of decades before Lita begins to sort out her thinking about who her mother was and is. One day she will develop greater self-awareness about who *she* desires to be and how those desires will differ and conflict with those of her mother. The guidance and support that exist in Lita's life outside of her family provide some sort of moral compass and

stable community for her. With this assistance, Lita has a chance
of developing a different style of parenting for her own children
despite what she has witnessed and experienced with Cynthia.
Lita's loyalty to and love for Cynthia will shape much of her
young adult life, but her relationship with Cynthia in the future
may be riddled with resentment and hostility. Their relationship
may be defined by an uphill battle to preserve the tie between
them, particularly as Lita grows in awareness that she dislikes
the person her mother has shown herself to be. As Lita grows
and becomes more self-aware (about age 30 in the life of most
women), she will look back on those early lessons and her mother's
example and wonder how that could have happened...what in
the heck was going on? Her mother will no longer be the saint
or the hero for whom Lita once yearned with an aching heart.
One day, there will be an indelible moment of reckoning when
some provoking incident will call forth the adult woman from
Lita's childhood illusions. When that happens, she will meet her
mother woman-to-woman for the first time.

Depending on your background, you may think this story
about Lita is an outrageous example of motherhood gone bad,
or you may think it pales in comparison to your own experience.
Whatever your perspective, the themes of: a) abandonment; b)
manipulation; c) disregard for one's emotional ties and overall
well-being; d) outright dishonesty; and e) selfishness present in
the Lita-Cynthia duo may be the same themes in your strained
relationship with your mother. However, these themes may be
expressed in different ways, even in ways that may be interpreted
as "virtuous" and doting maternal behavior. Your mother may
be one who refuses to see you as anything but perfect, so you're
never allowed to have a bad day, not even a bad hair day. As a
result, you feel cheated out of an honest relationship. Or perhaps
your mother incessantly worries and over-protects you, fighting
your battles long after you've resolved a matter. She may auto-
matically run interference for you even after you've acquired

skills, found trustworthy others and established sure footing, as though she *wants* you to experience fear, anxiety or distrust of others. Or your mother may have gratified your every need as though in service to royalty. In so doing, she then dominated your every thought, keeping you under her thumbnail out of selfish motivation to entice your dependence on *her* plans for your life. Alternatively, it could be that your mother is one who sets high standards admired by you and all who know her, yet she criticizes you for not living up to *her* standards while even comparing you to others without respect for your individuality. Or could it be that you're the one who has always been the parent in the relationship, responsible for your mother instead of vice versa? You long for a soft place to land, complete with the time-tested anchor of a mother's wisdom to nourish and refresh your soul for the journey ahead. Yet that anchor never materializes as you fight your way through the choppy waters of life without the benefit of "motherwit" as the old guard South calls it. Or maybe your mother has demonstrated such entitlement in her demands of your time and energies that you have felt you had to live two lives—yours and hers.

If you are forty*ish* or older, you may have come to terms with the sometimes harsh reality of who your mother is, but still struggle to maintain a respectful relationship with her. This may be due in part to her refusal to accept or even acknowledge your viewpoint or any emotional damage she may have inflicted upon you with or without awareness.

If you're thirty*ish*, you may be experiencing your first inklings of "something ain't right with my mom," but you can't quite put your finger on it other than just knowing that she GETS ON YOUR NERVES. Generally speaking, when you hit the pivotal age of 30, you have lived long enough to get a taste of life on your own. You've had a chance to see life through the lens of others' experience and make comparisons to your own life. The rose-colored glasses of childhood begin to lose their rosiness and you see others—including your mother—with fresh and objective eyes. That is, their imperfections, once unnoticeable or thought to be funny, unique, quirky or easy to overlook, can no longer be ignored or tolerated. They are now so real and in your face that you can almost reach out and touch them as you might be tempted to do when wearing 3-D glasses at the movies.

If you are twenty-five*ish* and under, you may still feel intensely protective of your mother and quite defensive toward anyone who tries to expose her flaws. Deep within, however, you may suspect that the feedback of others has a grain of truth to it that you'll need to review later.

Defending Mom's honor at all costs is generally expected in the African American community because so many of us have not had fathers who were emotionally or physically available to us. When Mama is your *only* parent, the thought of viewing her as less than perfect or loving, or of rebelling against her principles, is perceived as a gigantic risk to your survival. This idea of risk still looms largely in adulthood long after self-sufficiency as a stereotypic "strong black woman" (SBW) is established. Since Mama may be *all* you've ever had to depend on, expressing your anger toward her may not be a viable option. Hence, with great personal discomfort, the SBW may accept enduring responsibility for Mama and a "helpless" sibling(s) in exchange for Mama's comfort. Such chronic suppression of one's personal ideals and value system will be costly, even for the "invincible" SBW. The price paid may include feelings of depletion, isolation, resentment, self-doubt, and irrational anger in relationships or the world-at-large.

The reality is that your ability to thrive and grow into the woman God intended you to be, with a display of your unique gifts and talents for the world to see, depends on your ability, in part, to differentiate from "Mama 'n them" and minimize the related distractions. Failing to differentiate boxes you in to someone else's rules, standards and expectations in pursuit of dreams that are not your own. It's like trying to fit a square peg into a round hole; it simply will not and cannot fit.

The call to differentiate also demands an honest confrontation (mainly with self) of the ways you've allowed your life to be derailed because of even the *memories* of your mother's haunting shadow. These memories may leave you feeling inadequate or incapable of standing on your own convictions or compelled to forever blame her (perhaps secretly) for your life's failures.

Without the process of differentiation, you will always be the child in an adult body, hiding behind a false sense of dutiful obligation to go along with Mama in order to get along and keep the peace. Related to this, consider that the poetic Beatitudes of the Bible in Mathew 5:9 declare that "blessed are the peace-*makers*," which conveys empowering, *pro*active confrontation. It does not say blessed are the peace*keepers*, which conveys *re*active passivity and suppression. Also, keep in mind the shocking and controversial expressions of Christ in Matthew 10:34-36 when He states, "Do not suppose that I have come to bring peace to the earth. I did not come to bring peace, but a sword. For I have come to turn a man against his father, a daughter against her mother, a daughter-in-law against her mother-in-law—a man's enemies will be the members of his own household."

When I first read this as a new believer, I was dismayed and confused on how this type of language could be "Christ-like" and loving. After years of study and continual growth in understanding the character of God, in combination with seasoned life experiences, I now get it. I now understand that when you stand up for the truth as God has called you to it, you will see with startling clarity the necessity of departing from business as usual. Sometimes, this will cause friction with the people closest to you in life, including Mama. Ask any recovering addict who was introduced to drugs by family members, or any person who lost weight and adopted a healthier lifestyle while withstanding Mama's disappointment and even mockery over her refused fried chicken, or anyone who rebounded from bankruptcy "caused" by leaching family members; they will tell you how they *had* to depart from those near and dear who did not and could not support their new and improved vision for their lives. The meaning of this scripture should then become crystal clear as it relates to the concept of being set apart to honor God's plan in your sacred journey, a journey that you began alone and will end alone. By design, everyone will not be able to go with you.

So exactly what is this thing called differentiation? Glad you asked. Differentiation of the self is a concept developed by Dr. Murray Bowen, a widely studied psychiatrist credited with defining the field of family therapy in the late 1950s. His theories and clinical observations have given great depth to my professional and personal lives in the area of boundary-setting. He defined differentiation as the measure of one's emotional maturity, which can be discerned in how individuals draw distinctions between their thoughts and feelings, as well as distinctions between their connection to family or friends and their individuality.

At higher levels of differentiation, an individual is separate and responsible for him or herself while also accountable to and engaged with others. Capable of clear separation between thoughts and feelings in the midst of emotional events, the differentiated person is guided by a well-defined set of principles and goals. Therefore, a higher level of differentiation would make one less apt to get drawn into other's emotional issues and also less emotionally reactive in close relationships. Highly differentiated individuals tend to have few problems with anxiety in social situations and have more stable marriages than those who have low levels of differentiation. As an example, the highly differentiated wife will entertain honest feedback, even if negative, from her spouse about her family without anger and defensiveness.

At lower levels of differentiation, individuals are *under*-responsible for themselves and/or *over*-responsible for others, guided primarily by emotions or impulses with little to no reliance on thought (Wikipedia, Bowen). When asked what they *think*, they say what they *feel*; when asked what they *believe*, they repeat what they've *heard*. They either agree with everything or rebel against everything (Nichols and Schwartz 2004). They are generally consumed by relationships, leaving little energy for self-direction. Therefore, they tend to have more anxiety in social situations and more marital disruption than those with higher levels of differentiation (Popko and Dar 2001). The undifferentiated wife will *not* entertain negative feedback from her spouse about her family. She will more likely say something like, "Well that's my family and you just don't know them…you don't talk about my people, and I don't talk about yours…period!" Differentiation represents a fine balancing act between connectivity and independence. It is easier said than done, particularly for those who embrace a philosophy described by Dr. Beverly Green as "I am because *we* are" as many African Americans do (Green 1994).

I will talk more about differentiation later, but for now it must be said that whatever your attraction to the subject matter of this book, *Surviving Mama* is not intended to bash Mamas. I shudder to think of life without the African American mothers of yesteryear who held not only families, but entire communities, together throughout tumultuous times and violent attacks in this nation's history, particularly on African American men. I have nothing but love and admiration for these women of perseverance on whose mighty shoulders I stand. So the purpose is not to strike a heavy blow against Mama, nor is it intended to let those who are less-than-honorable Black fathers off the hook. It is intended to: (a) provoke honest thought and conversations with self and trusted others about how to navigate a strained relationship with a larger-than-life, "infallible" and almost iconic mother; (b) equip readers with greater self-awareness in updating their image of Mom, thereby allowing for an honest relationship with a flawed human being (such as we all are) versus an inflated image of Mom imprinted upon one's heart from childhood; (c) help readers give equal consideration to respect for Mom *and* respect for self; (d) provide the framework for a liberating adult mother-daughter relationship that minimizes knee-jerk reactions to the same drama; and (e) highlight those things about Mom that merit celebration based on careful consideration of her many lasting lessons.

The intended, though not exclusive, readership for this book is women who received what famed pediatrician and psychoanalyst Dr. Donald Woods Winnicott called "good-enough mothering." He used this to describe the appropriate weaning of a child away from its mother into independence and a social world in such a way that the child feels *loosened* from Mom and not *dropped* (Wikipedia, Winnicott). I use this phrase to mean that Mom's care appeared "normal" by Western standards in terms of education, clothing and basic provisions including meals, healthcare, birthday parties, holiday celebrations and acts of genuine love. Yet, somehow the adult daughter became increasingly conscious of the fact that interactions with her mother felt as incompatible as oil and water. The relationship, she came to understand, fell short of its potential due to Mama's dominance, excessive worry, thoughtlessness or self-absorption—all of which negatively shaped the daughter's view of herself in relation to others.

Some of you with a history of unusually harsh or abusive experiences with your mom may come to realize that the most prized lessons your mother imparted were how *not* to be and how to stretch yourself in *choosing* to love the unlovable. That can be a lesson more precious than silver or gold. As we begin this journey, please bear in mind that this book is not a substitute for the type of intense help that may be necessary for some who have endured trauma at the hands of Mama, but it may offer a stepping stone in the right direction. Readers may call 1-800-New-Life for information regarding more intensive resources for such recovery including a licensed therapist with a Biblical worldview near you.

Questions

1. Have I differentiated from my mother as evidenced by my ability to receive constructive feedback about her from caring others without getting defensive? What are her flaws that I have helped to enable? *I've never actually confronted those things that I felt slighted by but instead just made the "excuse" of "she wasn't ready to be a mother so..."*

2. What three positive lessons has my mother passed on to me? What are three negative aspects of her life examples or lessons that I need to discard or have already discarded from my own life? *Positive: Hustle, Keep my appearance together as a mom, free-spirited*

   Negative: manipulative, relationship issues, some selfishness in relationships

3. If I didn't have my mother to blame for some of my shortcomings or spend so much time warring with her, what would I need to confront in my own character and how could I spend my time more productively? *I don't think I blame her because I feel stronger for her non-involvement; sometimes I feel like thats the best thing that could have happened.*

4. What opinions did I develop, or what rights do I claim for myself, or what "rules" for life did I embrace for no other reason than they were my mother's teaching, but they really don't fit *my* life?_____

_____

_____

_____

_____

5. How have I rebelled against Mom's teaching just for the sake of rebelling?_____

_____

_____

_____

_____

6. Is my blind support of, or blind rebellion against, my mother working for me? _____

_____

_____

_____

_____

How so or how not? _____

_____

_____

_____

_____

References

Bible (New International Version).

Green, B. 1994. "African-American Women." In *Women of Color: Integrating ethnic and gender identities in psychotherapy,* edited by L. Comas-Diaz and B. Green, 10-29. New York: Guilford Press.

Nichols, M.P. and R.C. Schwartz. 2004. *Family Therapy Concepts and Method,* 121. Boston: Pearson A and B.

Popko, O.P. and R. Dar. 2001. "Contemporary Family Therapy." *Marital Quality, Family Patterns, and Children's Fears and Social Anxiety 23 (4): 465-487.*

Wikipedia. 2008. "Murray Bowen." Accessed July 2. http:// en.wikipedia.org/wiki/Murray_Bowen.

Wikipedia. 2008. "Donald Winnicott." Accessed July 5. http://en.wikipedia.org/wiki/Donald_Winnicott.

CHAPTER TWO

The Hand That Rocks the Cradle Rules the World...or Does It?

IT WAS THE DAY OF THE ANNUAL multi-family yard sale, and the participants (lifelong friends from college and high school) were as excited as young children on Christmas morning. Nobody expected to make a lot of money at these yard sales, and Lord knows they were a ton of work. However, everyone always looked forward to it as a day of fellowship away from husbands, commitments and household duties, and an excuse to sit on the front lawn and chew the fat. They relished all the giggling like school girls while the kids sold lemonade and homemade cupcakes without concern for the passing of time. It could have been a scene from a Norman Rockwell painting.

Most of all, yard sale day was a day in the "no-drama zone"—except for *this* particular day, when there was a scratch in the day's melody. One of the "vendors" had cleared out her deceased mother's house that year and had a king-sized canopy bed for sale. Few people showed interest until Marilyn, the mother of yard-sale participant Carlita, began to take serious interest in buying this luxurious bed for her seven-year-old granddaughter, Millicent. Marilyn decided she wanted Millicent to have the bed *despite* Carlita's protests, which were grounded in practical concerns such as Millicent's small and cluttered bedroom and the age-*in*appropriateness of the bed. In fact, Marilyn's face changed to one of glee as she realized she had an opportunity to irritate Carlita with her strong-willed decision to purchase this bed...*anyway*. The more Carlita protested, the greater the smirk on Marilyn's face became. "I've got my own money, and no one can stop me from buying this bed for Millicent if I want her to have it...I just want her to have it," quibbled Marilyn. The protests from Carlita only made Marilyn dig in further and pull out her money that much faster. Before you knew it, the bed was SOLD and arrangements were made for its delivery to Marilyn's own storage facility. Much to Carlita's disappointment, this altercation was typical of their exchanges and marked yet another round with Marilyn in the ongoing battle of the wills. After the purchase, Carlita shook her head in dismay; she never ceased to be amazed at Marilyn's indulgence of Millicent and her determination to undermine and control Carlita's parental decisions. Carlita, more of an old-school parent than her mother, was often aggravated by Marilyn's efforts to override her better judgment concerning Millicent's rearing. If Carlita instructed Marilyn to prohibit sweets for Millicent during a given time, Marilyn was sure to cut not one, but two pieces of cake for her. One such rebellious, sugar-loaded breakfast included a donut with chocolate icing, toast with jelly, fruit juice and honey-laden oatmeal. In addition to meal plan violations, Marilyn was also known for taking grandparent bragging rights to another level. She held sway over her "victims" with stories of Millicent's math talents and sure qualifications for the Mensa Society of geniuses. She once questioned with *seriousness* how any teacher could possibly teach Millicent because she was just *too* smart. Marilyn even insisted on taking Millicent's superior standardized test scores to show their hairdresser, much to Carlita's chagrin.

From a very young age, Carlita had thought that there was something about her mother that was...well...um..."special." Perhaps it started when her mother bought her a girdle at age nine, stating: "Your hips are too wide...and we gotta contain that." It wasn't long before the girdles replaced all of her panties, and they were the only undergarments Carlita wore despite the fact that she wasn't a big girl by any stretch of the imagination. It wasn't until Carlita was a teenager that she even suspected that other girls *didn't* wear girdles, and she was caught off guard by their surprised reactions to casual mention of hers.

The girdles were omens of other control measures to come. During "discussions," Marilyn often became so worked up in her need to drive home her point that once she got on her soapbox she'd *stay* on it without noticing that the teenaged Carlita had fallen asleep on her. Carlita often woke up to find Marilyn standing over her, still making her point with fire in her belly. These early antics of control and intrusion morphed into a lifetime of invasions, all designed to wield suffocating influence over Carlita's decisions, parenting style and comings and goings.

The tentacles of Marilyn's domination spread to all areas of Carlita's life. For instance, during college Carlita held a summer job at Neiman Marcus, where the high-brow shopped and Mozart wafted through the air. One day Marilyn barged into Carlita's workplace for the sole purpose of "fussing out" Carlita for using her forbidden hair dryer. Carlita had slipped and used it in a rush to finish grooming herself for work, knowing there'd be hell to pay if she was caught using *anything* of Marilyn's that had been designated off-limits. She just couldn't have fathomed her mother would travel all the way across town just to get her t-o-l-d.

All throughout Carlita's adult life, visits to her parents' house were met with Marilyn's immediate "show and tell" of her latest interests, including photographs, recent purchases and volunteer endeavors. Marilyn tooted her own horn in such a way that she alone controlled the direction of the conversation, making it as difficult to "dialogue" with her as it would be to interrupt a politician's filibuster. Few issues fell outside the purview of Marilyn's gripping control including her *opinions* regarding family members that she wanted others to accept as scientific *fact*. You see, Marilyn tried with mind-numbing tenacity to negatively influence Carlita's thoughts about certain family members, including a half-brother Carlita found out she had when she was in her late forties. This was a son born to Marilyn while she was in college who had been adopted by another family member and kept secret from Carlita. Once the true relationship was revealed, Marilyn discouraged any connection between the siblings. She frowned upon mention of their conversations and showed little to no enthusiasm for the siblings' growing intimacy. Most likely, the burgeoning relationship was a reminder to the image-conscious Marilyn of her transgressions while in college.

As Carlita grew in her understanding of the importance of honoring her mother, she often found herself as torn between respecting her mother and resisting her control as a man would be torn between saving his drowning daughter or his drowning wife. Carlita felt stifled as she realized that attempts at conversation with Marilyn about her controlling ways went nowhere FAST. She usually suffered through the oppression inherent in the relationship until she erupted with occasional, volcanic outbursts. Most of the time, she worked at accepting the reality that the relationship was what it was—taxing. She knew it could only progress if Marilyn loosened her clutches and let those around her soar with their unique opinions and attitudes. Carlita no longer hoped for such. She found herself rebelling or ignoring most things Marilyn said. Their relationship embodied a saying I once heard on a talk radio show: Rules without relationship equal rebellion.

This story of a mother's attempt to control her daughter's life is a common one, though the particular focus, severity and style of the control may differ. Perhaps your mother attempts to exercise control over your decisions with subtle and silent facial expressions, or maybe her style tends toward overt and loud directives of what you *must* do. She may guilt you into honoring her wishes by saying, "Well I don't ask you for much but..." or, "It's the least you could do for me." She may dominate your conversations with her until there is only one opinion that matters, and that's HERS. She may criticize your every move under the guise of trying to be helpful until you question your own judgment and concede to following her ways. Or your mother may kill you with kindness in such a way that it keeps you in bondage to honoring *her* wishes for *your* life because you worry that you would appear ungrateful by resisting her. Whatever the case may be, living under the pressure of your mother's control is as hefty a task as bench pressing a two-hundred-pound weight off your chest.

Any mother's attempt to micro-manage her daughter's life essentially says, "I don't trust you to make good decisions for your life and so let me ruin or stunt your development of any confidence by just telling you what you ought to do." It also says that Mama is too immature to accept that her daughter's reality may be different from hers, and that her daughter's pursuits may have different intentions than Mama envisioned. This mother can't handle the truth that her daughter is a never-before-seen and never-will-see-again creation of God and is therefore NOT at one with her. Examples include the stay-at-home mother who wants her very ambitious daughter to follow in her footsteps, or the professionally driven Hilary Clintonesque woman who wants her home-centered daughter to climb to greater corporate heights than she did. They may include the fashion-conscious, make-up wearing mother who rudely disapproves of her daughter's casual, make-up free, bohemian style. Or the ethnic-dressing, naturalist, India Arie-type mother who decries her daughter's attraction to a conventional, corporate look with chemically relaxed hair.

In pondering the meaning of control, I see a connection between the definition of control and the life of the controlled person. In an empirical study, the control variable is the variable that is held in a constant state without intervention in order to measure any changes in it as compared to the changes in those variables that did receive intervention. For example, the control group of patients in a study on a new cancer treatment will not receive the new treatment. The purpose of withholding the treatment is to see if those who did receive the new treatment significantly improved because of the *treatment* versus some spontaneous recovery that would have happened over time *without* any intervention. Like the control group, the controlled daughter is kept constant, never allowed to change for fear of messing up the mother's great experiment in cloning herself. It is an experiment destined to fail and even worse, an experiment that attempts to cheat God out of His magnificent plans for each of His creations.

When the individual purpose and creativity of one life is lost under the smothering influence, dominance or tyrannical control of another, I am reminded of the process of fusion: the act or procedure of liquefying or melting together by heat. Fusion was also a construct used in Dr. Murray Bowen's model of family therapy. He used the term to describe family dynamics where there was inseparable bonding, a sort of over-the-top togetherness, and discouragement of one's individuality/sense of self (Nichols and Schwartz 2004). For the purpose of this writing, I will use FUSION as an acronym to define a mother's misguided or maybe even pathological control. It is the process of "melting down" her daughter's dreams and goals for the purpose of shaping and molding them into dreams and goals that fulfill Mama's aspirations *only*. Hence FUSION will stand for

Fixated, Undermining, Self-absorbed, Intrusive, Obstructive and Never-ending.

Rebecca Walker (2008), daughter of famed writer Alice Walker, illustrates the inherent danger of FUSION in the mother-daughter relationship in her article "How My Mother's Fanatical Views Tore Us Apart." She writes:

> My mother's feminist principles colored every aspect of my life...When I got into Yale—a huge achievement—she asked why on earth I wanted to be educated at such a male bastion. Whenever I published anything, she wanted to write her version—trying to eclipse mine. When I wrote my memoir, *Black, White And Jewish,* my mother insisted on publishing her version. She finds it impossible to step out of the limelight, which is extremely ironic in light of her view that all women are sisters and should support one another....As a little girl, I wasn't even allowed to play with dolls or stuffed toys in case they brought out a maternal instinct. It was drummed into me that being a mother, raising children and running a home were a form of slavery. Having a career, traveling the world and being independent were what really mattered according to her....When I hit my 20s and first felt a longing to be a mother, I was totally confused. I could feel my biological clock ticking, but I felt if I listened to it, I would be betraying my mother and all she had taught me. When I met Glen, a teacher, at a seminar five years ago, I knew I had found the man I wanted to have a baby with. Gentle, kind and hugely supportive, he is, as I knew he would be, the most wonderful father....When I called her one morning in the spring of 2004 while I was at one of her homes house-sitting, and I told her my news [of pregnancy]

and that I'd never been happier, she went very quiet. All she could say was that she was shocked. Then she asked if I could check on her garden. I put the phone down and sobbed—she had deliberately withheld her approval with the intention of hurting me...I love my mother very much, but I haven't seen her or spoken to her since I became pregnant. She has never seen my son—her only grandchild. My crime? Daring to question her ideology.

In this example, Alice Walker is portrayed as **F**ixated on feminism as the very reason for breathing. She is depicted as one who attempts to **U**ndermine the desires of her daughter's heart to be a mother. She seems **S**elf-absorbed with her own pursuits and interests as the only priority that matters, and **I**ntrusive with her own opinions about the role of girls/women or the choice of one's schooling. She is portrayed as **O**bstructive in her apparent determination to deter the birth of any descendants and **N**ever-ending in her stance of self-righteousness for the cause of independent, unencumbered womanhood. Let me add here that I don't know Alice Walker and have never met her. I can no more judge her heart or the truth of her daughter's description than a blind man can see. So I make these statements based *solely* on what her daughter wrote in a *Mail Online* article. It is not my intention to choose one person to hold up as the poster child of controlling motherhood, but rather to provide examples that illustrate uglier aspects of ourselves or our mothers, aspects that cause unnecessary strain or rifts that blind us to the big picture.

Speaking of overlooking the big picture due to a controlling mindset, consider the biblical story in Luke 10:38-40 about Martha and Mary. They were the sisters of Lazarus, whom Jesus famously raised from the dead. As the story goes, Jesus and His disciples were traveling when a woman named Martha invited them to take a load off and visit her home for a while.

Throughout the visit, Mary sat at the feet of Jesus and listened to what He had to say. "But Martha was distracted by all the preparations that had to be made. She came to him [Jesus] and asked, 'Lord, don't you care that my sister has left me to do the work by myself? Tell her to help me!'"

Wow! Talk about a controlling spirit. *Martha* is the one who invited these people into her home in the first place—not Mary. Martha launches into over-achievement mode to make preparations (probably food) perhaps mirroring her namesake, Martha Stewart. Whatever these preparations are, we know they are not easy to pull together because the passage says that she is "distracted" by them. She is multi-tasking and pulling together several loose ends. Out of her frenzied need to impress, I suppose, she has the NERVE to make demands on her GUEST. She attempts to manipulate Jesus into seeing *her* perspective, when He is clearly just enjoying Himself. When Martha says, "Lord, don't you care…," she even makes the demand in such a way as to suggest that He is obviously seeing what she sees and has chosen to be uncaring in addressing it. Big Assumption. She also calls attention to herself as being the one who is self-sacrificing—the noble do-gooder—and not her sister Mary. Martha delivers the *coup de grâce* when she says to Jesus, "Tell her to help me!" Notice the exclamation point. She didn't just state this; she said it with gusto, alarm and excitement. I can just imagine Mary wanting to jump up and say in sister-girl style, "Oh no she did'ent."

Now Martha's demands—to put guests in the middle of a conflict and ask them to participate in vexing mediation—would be shameful to ask of *any* guest you have invited into your home. However, it's even more audacious for Martha to attempt to put the Savior of the world under her control, the one responsible for her domestic skills, her very breath and the beat of her heart. Furthermore, is there any reason Martha couldn't tell Mary herself what she thought of her? After all, she was sitting *right* there. The fact that she talks about Mary "behind her back" *in* Mary's face speaks volumes about Martha's character and hints at the jealousy she felt for the attention that Mary was enjoying in the company of their guests. Jesus confronts Martha with such simplicity, using very few words when He reminds her to stop sweating the small stuff. "Martha, Martha," the Lord answered, "you are worried and upset about many things, but only one thing is needed. Mary has chosen what is better, and it will not be taken away from her." (Luke 10:41-42). We see here that Jesus wants Martha to back up and to understand that this encounter is far more important than the perfectly orchestrated gathering. It's the relationship He is after, including the attention, the time, the fellowship, the conversation and just the presence of one with another. Everything else, including the do-good attitude and Martha's work-horse ethic, pales in comparison. The Bible doesn't say how Martha responded, but I imagine she stood there with egg on her face as she was called out for her rude behavior and reminded that her unattractive, condescending control was sucking the life out of the occasion. She was relentless in taking care of business but lost sight of the spirit of the event. She tried to then impose, or shall we say, *fuse* her ideas onto not only her sister but the Lord Himself.

Many of our mothers are Marthas. Many of *us* are Marthas. I will give Martha a pass for probably being well-meaning. Like Martha, most mothers are probably motivated by good intentions toward their daughters. However, some mothers may be so blinded by frantic attempts to *live* their daughters' lives *for* them that they lose awareness of the passions they could be killing, the burning desires they might be extinguishing, the growth they could be stunting, the ambitions they may be stifling, the conversations they are possibly thwarting, the wings they are likely clipping or the tentative heart-felt expressions they may be smothering into non-existence. Living a suppressed life or a life that has been contrived by another is not only "unfun" but is "unGodly," for not even God Himself forces His precepts on us. If God doesn't force us to choose Him, does any human have the right to force another adult to choose a certain path? *Giving* adults the freedom to choose is a loving act even if you know they're choosing unwisely. *Forcing* adults to live according to someone else's rules, desires or goals is oppressive and is therefore an *un*loving act. Such a weighty burden prevents God's gifts from manifesting in His precious daughters, and it attempts to lessen or undermine dependence on Him in favor of dependence on Mama. Having said that, the above is not written to give justification to rebel against lawful conduct, moral behavior or *everything* Mama or any other caring person says. There's no advice like that of a **well-balanced** mother. There's no wisdom like that of an experienced person who's gone before you. There's no more helpful conviction (other than the Holy Spirit) than that of a caring, non-controlling mother who gently reminds you of right from wrong and seeks to protect your best interests.

Consider this writing carefully and ponder the following questions to help increase understanding about whether you're controlled or convicted, undermined or unrepentant, disrespected or dismissive, demeaned or demanding. You decide.

Questions

1. Have I used my mother's control as an excuse for why my life is not on track? If I took her control or manipulation out of the equation, what character trait(s) of mine has worked against my dreams and goals? _____

   _____

   _____

   _____

   _____

2. What do I fear about being responsible for my own choices and setting my own boundaries? _____

   _____

   _____

   _____

   _____

3. If I didn't spend any time thinking about, rebelling against or complying with my mother's demands, what can I do with that extra time and effort to further my life today?

   _____

   Next week? _____

   _____

   Within one month? _____

   _____

   Within six months? _____

   _____

   Within a year? _____

   _____

   Within four years? _____

   _____

4. If I dared to resist my mother's smothering influence by just saying "No," what would happen first? _____

And then what?_____

And then what?_____

Is that the end of the world, or does it represent only a short-term discomfort for a long-term gain?_____

5. Have I possibly rebelled against genuinely wise counsel my mother has given me? Full of pride, have I hidden behind the "you're trying to control me" mantra that now seems like that of a silly teenager?_____

_____

_____

_____

_____

References

Bible (New International Version).

Nichols, M.P. and R.C. Schwartz. 2004. *Family Therapy Concepts and Method,* 374-375. Boston: Pearson A and B.

Walker, R. 2008. "How My Mother's Fanatical Views Tore Us Apart." *Mail Online.* Accessed April 8. http://www.dailymail.co.uk/…/How-mothers-fanatical-feminist-views-tore-apart-daughter-The-Color-Purple-author.html.

CHAPTER THREE

"If You're Gonna Worry, You Might As Well Not Pray; If You're Gonna Pray, You Might As Well Not Worry."

—unknown

PRISCILLA COULDN'T REMEMBER A TIME when her mother, Geraldine, had ever been at peace. Geraldine's world was defined by a fear of her own shadow. She was convinced that terror lurked around every corner, waiting to befall her or someone close to her at any moment. She had considered it her motherly duty to school Priscilla early on in the distrustful ways of others. Geraldine almost took pride in the fact that she had no real friends to speak of because after all, you can't trust people, not even your so-called "friends." Consequently, throughout her entire childhood Priscilla never had a babysitter because Geraldine had no support system from which to draw a trusted caretaker, and if she did, never would she have invited a "foreigner" into her home. Geraldine was unyielding in her determination to get Priscilla and others to worry about what *could* happen to them. Therefore, she acted as a self-appointed authority on events, places and circumstances that she'd *never experienced* in order to keep others abreast of the inherent dangers in every nook and cranny of life. She graciously volunteered to do their fretting for them, starting many of her sentences with, "It's so sad," or, "That's so scary…." So clear was the constant threat of danger to her that Geraldine wondered how others didn't see it as well. She often gripped the interior handle of the car door, as though holding on for dear life, any time Priscilla exceeded 40 mph or failed to begin braking when a car stopped a mile ahead of them. "Every time the doorbell rang she would dash to the back of the house as if she was running for her life," Priscilla recalled from her childhood. "It was not long before I began doing the same thing because that's what I thought was an appropriate response to a ringing doorbell."

On one occasion, Geraldine, Priscilla and Priscilla's husband went to Home Depot together, and Priscilla wandered off in the store for thirty minutes or so. Unbeknownst to Priscilla, Geraldine was frantic over her absence. With expressions as dramatic as any convincing trial attorney, she began to mount a campaign to incite panic in her son-in-law, Seth. "She may have been kidnapped or car-jacked!" she exclaimed. "Lord, what are we going to do?" she continued, her worry escalating into the stratosphere. She hoped Seth would buy into her unfounded fears and was disappointed when he didn't. When Priscilla resurfaced, none-the-wiser of Geraldine's hysteria, Geraldine gasped a loud sigh of relief, much to Priscilla's dismay. Seth filled her in on the details later. All Priscilla could do was groan about Geraldine's smothering cloud of over-protectiveness.

There was the time when Geraldine cautioned Priscilla with utmost concern that Priscilla's dog, Louie, had a ball in his mouth. Louie tried regularly to hustle someone to play a game of fetch with him by getting any passerby to notice he had the ball in his mouth. Because Louie *usually* had a ball in his mouth, Priscilla looked at her with puzzlement and a desire to understand the point of her statement. Geraldine went on to express her worries that Louie might swallow the ball and choke. Bear in mind this ball would be too large for a polar bear to swallow. When these moments of senseless worry and precaution crept into daily conversations, Priscilla re-experienced the burden of a lifetime of living under the "worryscope." With tightness in her chest, she remembered how Geraldine had answered most of her telephone calls when Priscilla was in her early twenties and fresh out of her childhood home, living alone for the first time. Geraldine routinely answered the phone with an expectancy of bad news. If Priscilla was not chipper in her tone *right* out of the gate, or if she happened to be chewing food and delayed in saying hello by two seconds, Geraldine prepared for the worst with hyperventilated breathing and an urgent bid for the bad news: "WHAT'S THE MATTER?"

As an older adult, Geraldine's worries were expressed like clock-work, so much so that Priscilla could almost tell time by how long it had been since the last statement of worry. For instance, anytime Priscilla lifted anything heavier than a can of soup, Geraldine cautioned her to be careful about injuring her back as Geraldine herself had done through years of gardening. Geraldine's rationale was that if something happened to *her*, it was bound to happen to *everybody*, and most of all to Priscilla. Geraldine's mantra was "been there, done that" used to affirm her qualifications for declaring the certainty of things going wrong. Every trip Priscilla made out of town was met with a compulsive admonishment that her easy style in interacting with others could get her into serious trouble; she needed to be careful to stay close to the hotel, lest she become prey for some wolf in sheep's clothing. This was all stated as if Priscilla, not a wild child who threw caution to the wind, had *just* mastered the art of crossing the street safely by herself after looking both ways.

The depth of Geraldine's worries was made as clear as fine print under a magnifying glass when she made a statement during casual conversation. Without any hint of understanding the magnitude of what she was communicating to Priscilla, she stated, "I don't go anywhere when you're out of town." When Priscilla inquired further about the meaning of this, Geraldine answered, "I mean I don't go *anywhere,* not to the grocery store, bank, post office, *anywhere,* because something might happen to me, and I couldn't call you for help." Priscilla sat back and just let that soak in. The message from Geraldine to her was more evident than it had ever been: "My life stops when you're out of my reach."

Don't get me wrong. It is a mother's right to worry at some time about *something* related to her child. It comes with the territory of bringing fragile, defenseless little ones into the world who depend on Mama to figure out and cater to their every need. A baby's ability to survive, to a large degree, is dependent on how adept the mother is at "smelling" danger, illness or threat and acting with the speed of a gazelle to avert potential harm to the baby. This ability is a God-given gift to mothers. However, like any God-given gift, when it lacks any restraint around its use the gift can become a curse rather than the blessing it was meant to be. In other words, the gift reaches a point of diminishing return and begins to work *against* the mother or child rather than *for* them. This is when motherly concern or uneasiness based on gut feelings or outright evidence crosses the threshold into unfounded, excessive and debilitating worry. It then becomes an intangible force to be reckoned with. You can't see it or touch it, but its stifling presence is undeniable and can shut down the best of them. In fact, one of Webster's definitions for worry is to pull, bite, or tear at something. That's it precisely! The threat of suffocating worry can: (a) *pull* one away from sharing intimate details of life with the worrier; (b) *bite* into the most exciting of times with projections of doom and gloom; or (c) *tear down* desires to adventure, explore and take risks that could serve to increase one's exposure and expand one's circle of influence.

Related to the concept of **(a) pulling away** from an intimate relationship, one individual whom I'll call Monica satirically commented, "All my mother knows about me is where I live and my phone number. She knows nothing else." Despite Monica's frequency of contact with her mother Elizabeth, and the fact that they shared similar interests and hobbies that gave the appearance of closeness, Monica felt as close to her mother emotionally as she did to a can of paint. For instance, Monica had not been able to tell Elizabeth that she was taking a chemistry class at a local university to polish her skills before starting a new job. She dreaded hearing her mother's excessive worries about the type of chemicals to which she might be exposed, or about the potential predator who might babysit her daughter while she was in class. Monica had learned as a child to proceed with caution in sharing even the most mundane of news with her mother. She worked doubly hard to keep big news undercover until absolutely forced to disclose it. The avenues or sources of worry were endless, and Monica knew it all too well. She had never been able to predict how far her mother's imagination would travel in order to generate a sense of panic. For these tried and true reasons, Monica had not even told her mother when she became engaged. She disclosed this only *after* the ring on her finger was discovered by another relative the next day while in the company of her mother.

A kindred spirit of Monica's, also striving to overcome maternal worry, piggybacked on Monica's sentiments. She stated, "When I was going through my infertility struggles, I couldn't tell my mother the unlikelihood of me being able to have a child until a year or so after the diagnosis...I couldn't run the risk of having to disrupt my own pursuit of healing and support in order to help my mother with *her* worries and grief for me. That would have added another whole layer of polluted thinking and confusion to deal with. Therefore, I said nothing to her while I endured the most traumatic time of my life."

Regarding **(b) biting** into someone's excitement with doom and gloom, imagine the predicament of thirty-one-year-old Gabriella when she excitedly announced to her mother Pauline that she'd been accepted into a PhD program at the University of Florida, a program prepared to give her more scholarship money than the university closer to where she lived with her mother. Instead of excitement and congratulations, worry dominated her mother's reaction like food dominates the thoughts of one hungering in a land of famine. Pauline bypassed the joy of the moment in favor of decrying the three or four hour-drive to the university. She blurted out in irritated tones, "Why would you want to go to school that far away?" as though Gabriella was leaving the continent and should know better than to do such a *foolish* thing. Much to Gabriella's dismay, Pauline continued, "That's so far away from me or anybody you know." Pauline's disapproval of the choice was palpable. As she drove with her on the day of the move to the new town, she protested even the travel route, citing dangers that were unfounded, at best, concerning rare sightings of alligators on the most direct route. Instead, she insisted on a longer, "safer," alligator-free route that doubled the length of the trip. As if these resistances were not enough, Pauline pursued the gold medal in how *not* to respond to a grown daughter's budding aspirations. She struck her final blow in dissecting Gabriella's choice of a cozy apartment as though it was a slum. "Why is the kitchen so far from the dining room… these rooms are so small…they could have put in new carpet… the closets are so tiny.…" On and on and on it went, thus **biting** a big chunk of joy out of Gabriella's new pursuit and teaching her a valuable lesson in what not to share with her mother. The irony is that Pauline had good intentions of concern for her daughter's safety and well-being, but her method of expressing her concern was as flawed as eating soup with a fork.

Taking a look at worry's ability to **(c) tear down** desires to explore and be adventurous, consider the trial of Andrea when she was exploring a jewel of an opportunity to study abroad in Spain for the summer months while in college. Andrea had visions of venturing into sidewalk cafes for lunch and having her ears tickled with the stimulating sound of foreign tongues. She looked forward to widening her lens and experiencing the world as others saw it. She knew that later in life there would be rare opportunity to travel abroad as career, marriage, bills and kids would become her priority. Andrea reported her plans to her mother, Josephine, with excitement that bubbled over like a shaken soda can just opened. She thought the idea might be a bit much for Josephine to swallow at first, but she hadn't quite anticipated how hard Josephine would push back. As you might have guessed by now, Josephine responded to Andrea's excitement with a resounding NO! She rattled off a list of reasons explaining why this was a bad and unacceptable idea, all related to the danger present at every turn for unsuspecting young women like Andrea. Andrea caved in, put up little protest, tucked her tail between her legs and went on with the routines of school and life. TEN YEARS LATER, a plane carrying students to Europe for a study-abroad summer program crashed and many of the students died. Josephine couldn't *wait* to call Andrea to tell her this is why she had cautioned her against this type of adventure. Josephine, oblivious to the passage of time and the statistical rarity of such an event, felt justified in her admonitions of ten years ago. Andrea was acutely aware of the disconnect between this event and her precious dreams as a wide-eyed student. She felt burdened by the reach of her mother's worry, which seemed to know no bounds or respect any statistical probabilities. Andrea still wonders, with deep regret some twenty-five years later, what might have been that summer when she was foot-loose and fancy-free.

Most of the time mothers who worry excessively probably have good intentions and may be oblivious to how much their worry drives a wedge between them and their daughters. The imagination of these professional worriers is over-active, quick and capable of creating scenes more vivid and detailed than any Hollywood producer could fathom. We see from the examples above how worry can pull, bite and tear down. However, worry is clever; it fools its perpetrators into thinking that the energy expended on worrying has the power to *prevent* harm, injury or accident. In that sense, "worry" becomes a sort of false god, attempting greater and greater control over its carriers until it blinds them to *likely* consequences and outcomes, allowing them only to see the most *extreme* circumstances as fact. With the following rhetorical question, Luke 12:25-26 reminds us that worry is certainly not God-like in its powers: "Who of you by worrying can add a single hour to your life? Since you cannot do this very little thing, why do you worry about the rest?"

In the mind of its carriers, worry becomes the hallmark sign of care and concern. It becomes a way of expressing love; worriers believe that their degree of worry equates with how deeply they care. However, this kind of expressed "care" actually short-circuits the plans and purposes of God because it constricts rather than widens, binds rather than liberates, suffocates rather than breathes life, stagnates rather than expedites, belittles rather than edifies and self-contains rather than multiplies a rich harvest in those who are here today and those who are to come. Paralyzing parental anxiety distracts a child from the delicate project of becoming a person. Instead, attention becomes prematurely diverted to the parents' needs, and authentic self-growth and development of the child is stunted. Thus, a daughter who chronically seeks to soothe maternal anxiety, making decisions and solving problems within the framework of minimizing or eliminating the risk of worrying Mama, may develop what Dr. D.W. Winnicott called "false self disorder." Please understand this is not a real disorder found in the *Diagnostic and Statistical Manual of Mental Disorders*, the "bible" for diagnosing psychological dysfunction. However, Winnicott used the term to describe a type of existence wherein the image of oneself as the distinct and creative center of one's own experience has been compromised or damaged (Mitchell and Black 1995). Hence, a daughter who perceives herself mainly as the object of her mother's worries, rather than a uniquely developing human being supported as such, may be a good candidate for false self disorder. This my be perceptible in a woman who is stumped by basic questions posed to her. Questions like "What do you like to do for fun?" Or, "What brings you joy?" Or, "What are your passions in life?" Or, "What are the desires of your heart?" She may give you that "deer-in-the-headlights" look as she responds, "I've never thought about that…I don't know."

It is important at this juncture to somewhat normalize an anxious style of mothering practiced by African American mothers, in particular, those who were raising children before the 1970s. Threats to their own lives and those of their children were legalized and/or acceptable practices by lawmakers and law keepers throughout this nation. I can recall stories of how my grandparents rigged up all types of playground equipment in the backyard of their home in Waycross, Georgia, including a makeshift merry-go-round. This minimized any temptation for my father and his two sisters to venture beyond their home for play and thus remain reasonably safe from predatory and murderous racists in the deep South of their era. In 1968 Grier and Cobb, two African American psychiatrists, introduced the idea of "culturally healthy paranoia" into clinical lore. It describes a protective and necessary reaction to racism (Ridley 2005) by a member of a minority group. It is a state of being that has characterized generations of parenting in caring African American families for good reason. Related to this, theologian Katie Cannon commented in *I've Known Rivers: Lives of Loss and Liberation* (Lawrence-Lightfoot 1995) that parents are obligated to pass on a healthy suspicion that is requisite for survival, a "jungle posture" that will empower their offspring to navigate America's minefields. Today, this healthy suspicion probably characterizes caring parents of *all* races given the myriad of opportunities for children to be preyed upon. However, the effects of this mindset on generations of the Black community may have produced quite the beast in some mothers already predisposed to hyper-vigilance in their search for potential danger. Geraldine was one such mother, who went into overdrive with her precautions, channeling the spirit of Glum, the character from *Gulliver's Travels* who announced every five minutes, "We're doomed!"

Now if worrisome motherhood pulls, bites and tears down, amongst other things, let's look at the power and influence of the "un-worried" mother. Probably one of the best examples is the mother of Moses (Exodus 2:1-10) who learned that a new king of Egypt had ordered every Hebrew newborn boy to be thrown into the Nile to drown. The king was concerned, or *worried* if you will, about the Hebrews' potential to outnumber the Egyptians and join with Egyptian enemies in a fight against Egypt, and then leave the country. Hence, he believed that Egypt might lose its slave labor and wealth if the Hebrews kept multiplying as they were.

Moses' mother did not lose precious time *worrying* about what to do. There is no reference to panicking, wringing of hands, pulling of hair, sweating bullets, losing sleep or being irritable and overly controlling. She put an ingenious and well-executed plan into action within three months that saved not only her son but eventually the entire Hebrew people from slavery. After she saw what a "fine child" Moses was—as the Book of Acts and the Book of Hebrews state that he was "no ordinary child"—she apparently couldn't bear the thought of harm coming to him, and she then purposed to hide Moses for three months. When that was no longer feasible, she went to Plan B, which represented her greatest act of "non-worrying." She placed him in a papyrus basket and floated him down the Nile. Now remember, the king's edict was to throw the baby boys into the Nile. Well Mama Moses threw him alright, that is, threw him right into a waterproofed basket that set sail nicely on the Nile. She cleverly "followed" the king's orders. Out of her concern, not worry, she sent Moses' sister to observe what happened to him. The sister observed that Pharaoh's daughter found him and, almost on cue, Moses began to cry when she opened the basket. Now what woman—other than those with abusive, murderous hearts—would turn away a crying, adorable, abandoned baby? Not even Pharaoh's daughter was able to do so, despite having full knowledge of her father's edict that these babies should be killed. Then the real genius of Mama Moses' strategy unfolded, perhaps preplanned or perhaps not. Moses' sister happened to make her presence known when Pharaoh's daughter discovered the baby. The sister shrewdly asked, "Shall I go and get one of the Hebrew women to nurse the baby for you?" When given an affirmative answer, guess which Hebrew woman she chose? You got it—none other than Moses' mother. To add ice cream, chocolate syrup and nuts to the icing on the cake, Pharaoh's daughter offered to *pay* Moses' mother to nurse him until he was perhaps a toddler (Wilke and Wilke 1993). Hence, Moses' mother not only saved her son's life by "giving him away" and trusting the outcome to God, but she received him right back and was *paid* to keep her own child until he was old enough to go live as a prince in Pharaoh's house. All of this was able to come about because of a "non-worrying" mother's demonstration of how to trust and love her child unto God.

If we break down the wisdom of Mama Moses' actions, we see that first, she recognized her limitations as a powerless slave. She knew she needed to buy herself some time to consider her options, so she did the only thing within her power, which was simply to hide Moses. I presume that she may not have had her plan's details worked out just yet, but she did what she knew how to do at the time with the available resources until further inspiration evolved.

Second, she decided to send Moses away from her. By giving him up, she knew he at least had a fighting *chance* at life; by keeping him she knew he had *no* chance. So she rolled the dice with a realistic understanding of the odds.

Third, she turned to those with powerful influence such as those of Pharaoh's household, even if by "planned chance" and even though they were her enemies. I imagine she had some knowledge of the direction in which she was sending the basket since the general vicinity of Pharaoh's neighborhood could not have been a secret any more than the White House's location is a secret.

Fourth, she enlisted help in her plan, namely her daughter, thereby avoiding the undue stress that results from attempting to handle life's stressors alone.

Fifth, in order to keep her life-saving scheme under cover she must have kept her cool and put on the best of poker faces when asked to nurse her own son.

The rest of the story, as they say, is history. Moses received the kind of rearing and instruction, along with the opportunity to live with royalty in Pharaoh's house, that he needed later to command authority over hundreds of thousands of enslaved Hebrews. He became such a powerhouse that thousands of years later, you can pull an illiterate street person out from under a rock and ask him or her: "Who was Moses?" The answer will be: "Didn't he set the Hebrew slaves free?" This is what "worry-free" motherhood can do for a child and for those who will benefit from association with that child. Instead of pulling people apart as we saw in earlier examples of worry-*filled* mothering, "worry-*free*" mothering releases the child to soar to great heights, which may unite and influence generations to come, as seen in the story of Moses.

Yet another potent example of "worry-free" mothering is the story in 1 Kings 3:16-28, a story that depicts the matchless wisdom granted by God to King Solomon in answer to his prayer request. King Solomon presides over a dispute between two prostitutes, both mothers and both living in the same brothel. The baby of one of the mother's died, supposedly because his mother accidentally laid on him. The dead baby's mother then took the other woman's baby while she slept and placed the dead baby near her breast. She then proceeded to pass the live baby off as her own.

As you might imagine, an irresolvable argument ensued, and the case had to come before King Solomon for adjudication, a sort of Supreme Court of the day. King Solomon gave an order to "cut the living child in two and give half to one and half to the other." Upon hearing this, the real mother pleaded, "Please, my lord, give her the living baby! Don't kill him!" The fake mother said, "Neither I nor you shall have him. Cut him in two!" Then the king gave his ruling: "Give the living baby to the first woman. Do not kill him; she is the mother."

King Solomon, in his brilliance, understood that a mother must sometimes surrender her pleasure in and possessiveness of her child in order to let that child live and thrive. Here again as seen with Mama Moses, the paradox is that in choosing to release the child, the mother gained the child for keeps. "Worry-free" mothering favors the best interest of the child over EVERYTHING else. The victorious mother in 1 Kings essentially communicated: "I'd rather live without you and release you to the unknown than for one precious hair on your head to be harmed." Her selfless actions kept the child from being torn apart (though that wasn't ever Solomon's intention). The story brings into sharp focus the necessity of being prepared to risk losing a relationship in order to save it and bring forth its greatest good, intimacy and growth.

Could your relationship with your mother or your life's purpose have been sabotaged or short-circuited by worry? Consider the following questions:

Questions

1. Did I buy into my mother's excessive worry at some point and allow it to limit my potential? Minimize my dreams? Think of every risk as a reason to forgo opportunities? If so, name at least one specific example:_____

_____

_____

_____

_____

2. When have I withheld stressful news from my mother in order to avoid having to emotionally support *her* through *my* crisis when in actuality I could use the support myself?

_____

_____

_____

Who can I recruit for support that I might have overlooked out of years of conditioning myself to be strong all by myself?_____

_____

_____

_____

_____

3. How do I respond to my mother during one of her worrying episodes? Be specific. And how is that working for me (to quote the question made famous by Dr. Phil)?

_____

_____

_____

_____

_____

4. What was my proudest moment in standing on my own convictions in opposition to Mama's irrational worries or guilt-inducing tactics? What keeps me from doing more of that? _____

_____

_____

_____

_____

_____

5. What ONE action can I take in my next smothering or hovering encounter with Mama that will minimize or eliminate the impact of her excessive worries on my life?

_____

_____

_____

_____

_____

References

Bible (New International Version).

Lawrence-Lightfoot, S. 1995. *I've Known Rivers: Lives of Loss and Liberation*, 644. New York, New York: Penguin Books.

The Merriam-Webster Dictionary. 2004. Springfield, Massachusetts: Merriam-Webster, Inc.

Mitchell, S. and M.J. Black. 1995. *Freud and Beyond*, 124, 209-210. New York, New York: Basic Books.

Ridley, C. 2005. *Overcoming Unintentional Racism in Counseling and Therapy*, 64. Thousand Oaks, California: Sage Publications.

Wilke, R. and J. Wilke. 1993. *Disciple: Becoming Disciples Through Bible Study*, 36. Nashville, Tennessee: Abingdon Press.

Chapter Four

A Chip Off the Old Block...
or Maybe Not

Forty-five years of age, never married and childless, Megan was leaving the haven of her parents' suburban home once again after a multi-year retooling of her financial affairs. She had experienced a temporary setback after purchasing her first home. Unfortunately the forty-year old wood-framed house and the gentrifying urban neighborhood proved to be eerily unsafe. After the sun retired, there were unsettling sounds throughout the house that raised goose bumps of suspicion and the nauseating sensation of being preyed upon. Outside of the house, an unfamiliar culture of street dwellers who materialized only at night blended in with the constant din of traffic and disturbing altercations. Music, if you want to call it that, blared from passing cars, loaded with the boom BOOM, boom BOOM, boom BOOM of "gangsta" rap followed by the vibrations of speakers barely able to carry the volume. All of the disturbing sounds combined to form a white noise that became the backdrop of Megan's existence in that home.

In addition to the insistent noise, smells from greasy local restaurants permeated the air. And then there were the unrelenting stares of her stalker-like neighbor. Her suspicions of him were heightened when he startled Megan with a greeting from his bedroom window as she arrived home late one night and exited her car to retrieve groceries. He called out, "Go ahead and get your groceries. I'm watchin' to make sure that n-o-o-o-o-t-h-i-n's gonna happen to you." She felt grimy just hearing his voice, and she thought, "Who died and left you in charge of the safety patrol, and furthermore who's watching you with your sleazy self?"

Instead of the sanctuary she yearned for her home to be, Megan found this place to be like the valley of the shadow of death, engulfing her and smothering her very being with creepy vibes. She existed under this shadow for two and a half years until she could no longer stomach the queasiness. Casting aside all concerns for credit scores and asset protection in favor of physical and mental preservation, Megan abandoned the home under the cover of darkness. As she ran back to the familiarity of her parents' home, she felt as though she was fleeing for her very life.

However, she was acutely aware that she was jumping out of the frying pan and into the kettle. Megan's parents welcomed her back gladly into their comfortable home, letting her know she could stay for as long as she needed to recover financially after foreclosure and plan her life. Nevertheless, Megan knew all too well that a pit stop at her parents' house, however brief, would come at a cost.

The main problem was that Earlene, Megan's mom, was under the illusion that Megan delighted in spending *every* waking moment with her. Earlene felt so close to Megan that frequently, she let her guard down and verbally unleashed all her hopes, dreams and fears for her only daughter, however belittling, however dismissive of her individual strides, however superficial, however toxic. Earlene had mapped out Megan's entire life, from the crib onwards. This was easy for her to do because it was really the same template Earlene had for her *own* life when, as a young woman, she had the proverbial hope chest brimming with grandiose dreams. As the reality of life dimmed Earlene's bright visions, she projected her hopes and aspirations onto Megan. Thus, Earlene had a specific future planned for Megan, and she was bound and determined to make sure that plan was emblazoned on Megan's forehead as indelibly as a cowboy's brand on his cattle. Sadly, it didn't take long for the young Megan to hone in on the fact that Earlene began to grieve the loss of the *contrived* Megan when the *real* Megan grew up and fell short of her vision.

As early as age seven, clues of Earlene's expectations for Megan's development began to surface. One sweltering Saturday evening while Earlene stood over the stove, heating the "hot comb" used to straighten Megan's soft and full head of hair, Megan was bewildered by Earlene's murmurings about the quality of her hair. Megan heard Earlene's sorrowful lament, whispered under her breath with every downward stroke of the smoking comb: "I just thought your hair would have turned out better than this. Your dad has such a nice grade of hair." Megan struggled to comprehend what Earlene meant. For reasons she couldn't quite understand, she felt bad about having displeased her mother, the exact opposite of her seven-year-old intentions. Megan discerned that something about her hair, as it was, proved to be flat-out disappointing to Earlene. Even today, Megan's return from the hairdresser serves as an immediate invitation for Earlene to comb her fingers through Megan's fresh "do" and offer reminders that "gray hair is coming in riiiiiight there," followed by scolding questions of whether color was applied to "cover that up."

Megan's hair was not Earlene's only obsession. She was also obsessed with body image. During Megan's return stint at home, Earlene once laid out on her bed a surprise gift for Megan with confidence that her thoughtful generosity would be received as a welcomed blessing. "I left something on the bed for you… you can start wearing these now…it's just something that runs in the family…don't worry, just get control over it now." Much to Megan's chagrin, she discovered Earlene had bequeathed her personal collection of used girdles from the 1970s to Megan. Megan didn't know whether to thank her for what were hopefully good intentions or cut those girdles up and throw them in Earlene's face.

Earlene's preoccupation with the bodies of Megan's friends was another subtle reminder of her intense focus on Megan's body image. RIGHT after hello, one friend in particular was always greeted with an immediate assessment of her persistent slenderness and serious questions about how she maintained that size, as if the responses would somehow alert Megan to what she should, would or could do. Megan would think to herself, "Should I ask her to make me an appointment for a tummy tuck, liposuction and a face lift while we're on a roll here… surely the potential risk of death or permanent damage to my body is worth it, right?"

As Megan's prospects for marriage dimmed, Earlene acted as though she could *smell* a potential husband for Megan at the mere mention of a man who happened to have two legs and could breathe on his own. You see, in Earlene's mind, marriage and motherhood were the only secure roads for a respectable woman. So Earlene would wait with abated breath for a report on marital potential every time Megan so much as went to lunch with a guy. Oh, and let's not forget the baby and bridal showers they attended together. These events had become as painful as having fingernails pulled out one at a time. Every time Megan and Earlene celebrated the arrival of a new baby or an upcoming marriage, Megan knew to brace herself for Earlene's palpable anxiety. "I can't wait until you give me a grandchild," Earlene would quiver. Megan would think to herself, "Uh...don't you like...um...already have five grandchildren from my brothers?" Those grandchildren, Megan learned, didn't really count like grandchildren from *her* would count someday.

There was just no ceiling on Earlene's intrusions and obsessive thoughts on what was taking Megan so long to marry and become a mother. She was even meddlesome enough to question Megan's sexual orientation. "I had a dream," volunteered Earlene nervously one morning over breakfast, "that you were a lesbian...you haven't brought a man by the house in so long. You don't like women, do you?" Leaning over her coffee cup, Earlene searched Megan with the frightened eyes of a hen surrounded by foxes. Megan just stared back at her mother, paralyzed. Her lips were pursed to respond, but she couldn't give voice to her racing, bewildered thoughts. She decided the question was hardly worth honoring with a response given the spirit and tone in which it was asked. The two continued on with their breakfast in painful silence. Megan allowed only the escape of a long, exasperated sigh.

During her return tour of home, Megan put up with having to relive the in-your-face jabs and comments, in addition to belittling questions and gestures. Finally the glory day came for Megan to move out again. This time, it was for good! With the glee of an eager child preparing for her first day of school, Megan began to move a chair out of the garage, which was now chock-full of items she'd been stockpiling over the years in preparation for this long-awaited moving day. Megan reflected on how the brief pit stop she had planned to make at her parents' home had morphed from one year into four years, ten months, three weeks, two days and five hours. As she became lost in her thoughts while still maneuvering the chair out of its cramped space, the garage door began to slide down unbeknown to Megan. BAM! The door hit her so hard on the crown of her head that she swore she heard her skull crack. That crack was not just a physical crack, but an emotional crack that opened a floodgate of tears that burst forth with the ferocity of Niagara Falls. The garage door hit a nerve, inciting Megan to cry for every blessed thing that had happened in that home in which she had been raised and returned to by default. She cried for the little girl who became the woman whose acceptance by her mother was questionable. She mourned for the girl whose image just as it was and whose pure heart and awesome contributions to others would always pale in comparison to Earlene's mirage of who she thought her daughter should have been. The tears flowed and they flowed, and they poured and they poured and then they poured some more and then still more.

Megan experienced a flood of memories of events that had left her having to earn approval and perform her way into acceptance. Often as a small child she endured unending chores of cooking, laundry and cleaning while her mother lay helplessly in bed "ailing" and screeching her demands. Megan's domestic performance as a child would have given even a grown woman a run for the money. She had felt a bit Cinderella*ish*, but unlike Cinderella, she wasn't the stepchild. Unfortunately, Megan created disappointment by making the "sad mistake" of being born in her own image and likeness—as God intended—and not Earlene's.

Megan thought she might never stop crying, her heaving was so intense. Afterward, she felt the tears had cleansed her in preparation for her exodus to her promised land of self-acceptance. This cleansing included vows to liberate herself from that house, what transpired there and the hurtful put-downs from a "well-meaning" Earlene. Earlene, on the other hand, was off and running to create a new image of Megan, centered on the "grand house" in which Megan now lived. It was a comfortable home for sure, well appointed with Megan's tasteful yard sale finds and Craigslist bargains. However, it was hardly a palace worthy of an Arabian sheik as Earlene would have others believe. Relatives told Megan, "We gotta come see your house...your mama can't stop talking about it and telling us it is a MUST-SEE home." Earlene embellished the reality of Megan's cozy abode with descriptors that were unrecognizable to Megan. Would the truth of her life ever just be enough on its own? She concluded, "Probably not." Earlene had always seemed to take pride in her attempts to illustrate to Megan how life, love and appearance *should have* gone for her.

Trying to live up to the "shoulds" of life, self-imposed or other-imposed, is generally unproductive and self-defeating. David D. Burns, M.D., author of *The Feeling Good Handbook*, states that "should statements" directed at the self lead to guilt and frustration; when directed at someone else, they generally lead to anger and frustration. These "should statements" don't work in trying to change self or others because they usually produce rebellion and an urge to do just the opposite. Think of those who diet as often as the changing seasons, and you'll hear him or her say, "I *shouldn't* eat that cookie," in a voice muffled by cookie-stuffed-in-mouth before completing the sentence. Hence, trying to live up to a certain ideal, or nagging someone else into doing so, is referred to by Burns as the "shouldy" approach to life. Say that aloud, and you'll hear the inherent crap.

Earlene has great difficulty understanding where she ends and Megan begins. She has attempted to have an enmeshed relationship with Megan whereby they could move and think as one. The enmeshed relationship thrives on the belief that one set of desires, hopes and dreams exist between two people with little to no separation or independence in thought. Just like fusion, defined earlier, it is the opposite of the differentiated relationship discussed in Chapter One. Following this train of thought, Earlene believes that what *she* wants, Megan must surely want as well. The stumbling block for Earlene is that it takes two to tango, and Megan has been unwilling to engage in the enmeshment with utter abandon. Has Megan been impacted by it and at times engulfed by it throughout her life's journey? Certainly, in an exhausting, uphill-battle kind of way. Did she surrender to it completely? No, and while she has plenty of battle scars to show for Earlene's attempted fusion, she has persevered to have her own voice. So Earlene's efforts to mold Megan in the image and likeness of herself did not manifest the desired results for Earlene. Instead, the result has been the presence of friction and resentment as familiar companions in this mother-daughter dyad, the likes of which Earlene probably won't ever fully recognize or comprehend. Earlene is so convinced that her desires for Megan are righteous and therefore must be imparted as the only possible truth. Her intentions may come from a good place, of wanting the best for her daughter. However, what is considered "the best" involves only one opinion: Earlene's. Thus, daughters in Megan's position are cheated out of really being known by their mothers, even though they may spend a lot of time together.

A mother's over-involvement with her own vision for her daughter's life likely represents two sides of the same coin. One side of the coin may have originated from the mother's deep disappointments about the shortcomings of her own life. She may have managed those disappointments or kept them from destroying her by purposing to steer her daughter away from the mistakes and oversights she made at *all costs* without even realizing her overbearing nature. She may have relieved herself and aided her emotional survival long before her daughter was born by clenching on to a belief that, "One day I'll have another chance through my children through whom I can celebrate my delayed or preferred achievements vicariously." This belief may exist outside of the mother's conscious awareness, making it hard for a daughter's protests to register with her. In the best case scenario, a mom desires to "protect" her daughter from costly mistakes or setbacks. Any good mother does this *within reason.*

After all, how evil would it be for a mother to stand by, knowing that her daughter is headed toward danger, destruction and despair, and yet provide absolutely *no* counsel? However, when the counsel becomes dogmatic the other side of the coin surfaces. That side is anchored in a more willful and toxic dismissiveness such as is characteristic of pronounced narcissistic traits or full-blown narcissistic personality disorder.

Narcissism is a personality trait or, in some cases, a disorder named for the Greek hero Narcissus, who was renowned for his beauty and who was eventually punished for his cruelty to those who loved him. That punishment was his paralyzing transfixion on his reflection in a pool of water. He stayed there forever gazing upon himself until he perished. At its root, narcissism tells its possessor, "Your opinions are superior to the opinions of others, and no one is in your league of accomplishment, style, intelligence, position, talent, skill, understanding, desirability, success, looks or 'specialness' in whatever category of life—even illness." Moreover, narcissists believe that others are privileged to be in their company or in service to them. Certainly, everyone wishes they were living *their* life or following *their* advice, including God, they believe. Furthermore, narcissism tells its possessor, "Your image and the essence of you is so distinguished that it commands unusual attention and cuts a path that surely others will want to follow, admire or duplicate." Narcissistic people present such "special" cases, insights, experiences or knowledge that others should be compelled, they believe, to treat them as top priority worthy of irrational sacrifices in time, energy, money and personal desires. Narcissism is complex and may manifest in a myriad of obvious or subtle ways such as: a) the mother who defends a husband or boyfriend known to be abusing her daughter because he's "good" to her; b) the mother who habitually and abundantly praises her daughter only when others are watching and who returns to negligence or put-downs when nobody is taking notice; or c) the mother who is helpless and dependent "in her mind" and makes "demands" on her daughter either overtly or in a tone as sweet as the sound of a baby's babbling. This mother requires special attention and consideration by her daughter at *unreasonable and repetitive costs* to the daughter. These latter two examples come close to describing Earlene's brand of narcissism.*

Now let us direct our attention to a powerful example of the "un-narcissistic" parent. It is taken from a familiar biblical story that underscores the unmistakable and radical calling on a parent to separate his or her mission from that of the offspring. I'm referring to Abraham's assignment from God to sacrifice (that is, kill) his long-awaited and beloved son, a son not born to him until he was one hundred years old. Nary a sane and loving soul today could fathom doing such a thing to a precious child—even for God. Can you imagine explaining the attempted murder of your child to the Department of Children and Family Services by saying, "God commanded me to do so?" Upon close examination, we see that Abraham really couldn't fathom God's request either, as evidenced by his statement to his servants when he came upon the place where God had directed him to make the sacrifice. Abraham instructed, "Stay here with the donkey while I and the boy go over there. We will worship and then we will come back to you" (Genesis 22:4-5). Notice the phrase "*we* will come back." With the use of that one pronoun, we, Abraham is saying, "I'm coming back *with* my son. I don't know how this thing is gonna work out, but I know the heart and character of God. I trust Him, and I'm willing to pursue this to find out where it's going to take me."

The story is well known and is overflowing with lessons of all kinds. For the purpose of illustrating what is relevant for this chapter, I will focus on the lesson that screams loudest to me: a mother's vision of her daughter's future is not always one and

---

* For further reading on the impact on the child of a narcissistic parent, please explore *Help! I'm In Love With A Narcissist* by Steven Carter and Julia Sokol.

the same as God's. It is, at the end of the day, *His* vision that matters most, period. Therefore Abraham, and indeed any parent, is expected by God to denounce any temptation to make an idol of a son or daughter. In the biblical example, the call for Abraham to sacrifice Isaac erased any confusion that might have occurred with regard to worship of God versus worship of the long-awaited Isaac. I perceive God to be saying, "Not even your precious little one will be an acceptable excuse for knocking me off the pedestal as your number one priority." That's one of the perks of having the creative power to breathe life into someone; God gets to make requests of us and have plans for us that serve *His* purpose, which is bigger than anything imagined by the limited human mind. Obedience to His vision and release of one's own vision is the hard part, but it defines the path to abundant fruitfulness in life. By surrendering to God and trusting that He must know what He's doing since He is God 'n' all, Abraham proved himself worthy of the tremendous call to leadership on his life. Today, Abraham is renowned in all three of the world's major religions: Judaism, Christianity and Islam. Thus, God made good on the meaning of Abraham's name, Father of Many. Abraham's far-reaching authority was founded upon *release* of his hopes and dreams for Isaac and *submission* to God's perfect plan.

Though Abraham made his share of mistakes and sinned like everyone else, he will always be known for his lesser concern for interfering with Isaac's destiny and his greater concern for following God's plan and purpose for the child of promise. Abraham's story contains an epic model of faith and obedience that illuminates the importance of getting out of God's way and surrendering to His will. It's a powerful lesson for mothers to remember when shepherding the next generation into womanhood with choices, looks, style, decisions and careers that might not turn out like Mama envisioned.

Questions

1. Have I sought to live up to my mother's image of who she thinks I should be, thus squandering the use of my God-given talents and skills in order to please her exclusively? If yes, how so? _____

   _____

   _____

   _____

   _____

2. Have I allowed my mother to "should" me to death and am I now burdened with guilt over my mother's disappointment in me in ways that I know are irrational? Name an example:_____

   _____

   _____

   _____

   _____

3. Do I seek out people in my life who affirm who I am or am I constantly trying to win the approval of self-absorbed people, like my mother, by giving too much or being someone for them that I'm really not? Who is affirming the *real* me?

   _____

   _____

   _____

   _____

   Who am I caving in to? _____

   _____

   _____

   _____

   _____

4. Who am I really serving in life: Mama or God? _____
_____
_____
_____
_____

References

Bible (New International Version).

Burns, D. 1999. *The Feeling Good Handbook.* New York, New York: Plume Books.

CHAPTER FIVE

"When I Was a Child, I Talked Like a Child...When I Became a [Woman], I Put Childish Ways Behind Me..."

— 1 Cor.13:11

or Did I?

GABRIELLA, ALSO KNOWN AS GABBY, couldn't believe what she was hearing. Was that...*crying* she heard coming from her mother? It was first thing in the morning. "What could have happened?" she wondered as she made this routine wake-up call to her mother, Esther. Esther was one who *LOVED* sleeping late and thought of it as one of those inalienable rights the Constitution *must* have been talking about. Since Gabby was getting up extra early these days to exercise, she'd been serving as Esther's alarm clock. Every day she helped her mother to jump-start her preparations for her work as a nanny for an adorable toddler, the daughter of very busy parents with unpredictable schedules. This day, the morning routine was interrupted by Esther's unexpected sniffles and cracking voice, making Gabby's brow furrow. She silenced herself to make sure she heard what she *thought* she was hearing. Sure enough, she had heard right. Through her sobs, Esther was pleading, "Don't make me go...I don't want to go...it's so-o-o hard."

Gabby was growing accustomed to Esther's predictable whining and feigned helplessness. However, it took Gabby a minute to recover from the dismay she felt at hearing this "grown-behind woman" cry about going to work in the same manner that a toddler might cry at having a toy taken away. Gabby gave her characteristic response peppered with dry, matter-of-fact humor. "Well I think, Mama, if Harriet Tubman and Sojourner Truth found a way to do what they did, you can get up and drive across town in a plush car to a plush home to work in an air-conditioned climate catering to the needs of a precious little girl who brings you great joy...thank God Harriet 'n' them made a way for us."

From an early age, Gabby had always sensed that she was somehow tougher than her mom and that they were cut from cloths as different as delicate tulle (used for bridal veils) is from sturdy canvas. Gabby had an independent, common-sense grounding and an easy way with a network of friends and associates that allowed her to move through life with unshakeable confidence and get things done efficiently. As relaxed as she was in her interactions with others, she always maintained a keen awareness of people, places and circumstances that rivaled the hyper-vigilance of the Secret Service. She was as "shrewd as snakes and as innocent as doves" (Matthew 10:16).

As far as Esther was concerned, Gabby's savvy life skills were just what the doctor ordered after her divorce from her second husband, Clarence. Unfortunately for Gabby, Esther's dependence on her—as well as others who she perceived to be stronger or more knowledgeable than her—became increasingly noticeable and draining. In addition to Esther's annoying clinginess, Gabby had to wrestle with the predictable complaints that were sprinkled throughout Esther's conversation with the consistency of a leaking faucet, dripping just often and loud enough to prevent sleep. On the worst of days, Gabby felt that no military operation could hold a candle to Esther when it came to subtle and stealthy torture.

It was during her college years that Gabby began to notice how her mother's complaints shifted according to whatever was convenient for her at the moment. Whenever circumstances, jobs and other people in her life became inconvenient, complaints were born, signaling a change in Esther's loyalties towards, and opinions of, others. This was especially true in the case of Clarence, Gabby's beloved stepfather, whom Gabby had grown to love over the decades with as much endearment as she had for her natural father. Gabby easily recalled Esther's persistence in getting her, a young girl, to embrace Clarence over her natural father whom Esther had divorced when Gabby was two. Esther persevered in encouraging this stepdaughter/stepfather alliance without respect for Gabby's biological father to whom Gabby remained close until his death when she was thirteen. Clarence had arrived as a knight in shining armor rescuing the damsel Esther in distress, and she wanted everybody on board with this new program. He was the good guy from a good family who was good to his new wife and stepdaughter in terms of reliability, provisions, work ethic, household maintenance and steadfast commitment, even to his in-laws whom he nursed on their deathbeds.

It is important to understand Esther's background. As a young woman she made mistakes that hampered what could have been a smooth launch into adulthood. She became pregnant while a sophomore in college. Subscribing to her parents' wishes, she dropped out of college and married the father. Two years later, she was an undereducated divorcee single-handedly raising a child. These were foreign times for Esther, whose parents had doted on their baby girl as though she was royalty.

Clarence was looking to settle down when he entered Esther's floundering life, and he was all too eager to be a provider and protector for Esther and Gabby. Under Clarence's careful and predictable watch, Esther's life was transformed into one as mindless as that of a nursing baby, which by the way, Clarence and Esther gave birth to some four years later. The relationship was a good fit until Gabby went to college, and the intensity of Esther's child-rearing years drew to a close. That's when Gabby first noticed the shift in Esther's chatter about Clarence. Much to Gabby's confusion, he had now become the source of all Esther's unhappiness and the focus of her complaints. Esther actively sought Gabby's agreement that Clarence was the unequivocal reason for Esther's unhappiness. The more Gabby retreated from the venom hurled at Clarence, the louder Esther protested and proclaimed her bondage to a life of discontent, with dramatic diatribes that the Academy Awards needed to know about. Esther was practically wearing sackcloth and ashes in her attempt to make Gabby notice her misery as Clarence's pampered wife. The more Gabby refused to participate in Esther's "pity parties," the more the emotional distance grew between them until a chasm was created that was impossible to ignore. For sure Gabby loved her mother, and she knew her mother would give her the shirt off her back. However, the weight of Esther's "pitifulness" was a heavy load for Gabby to carry. Without a career, hobbies or interests to preoccupy her attention, Esther relied more on her daughters for fun and excitement as she continued to spew put-downs of Clarence in front of Gabby or anyone who happened to be within earshot of the tongue lashing. This infuriated Gabby and fertilized the weeds growing in their garden of mother-daughter harmony, choking out the rich harvest that should have been theirs after years of closeness.

It wasn't until Esther finally divorced Clarence in search of "something more," that things took a nose dive between Esther and Gabby. Esther found herself in virgin territory. As she approached age sixty, she was a stranded soul *completely* on her own for the first time—no parents, no husband, no boyfriend and no children at home. Everyday problem-solving and household management became as daunting for Esther as climbing Mt. Everest without a guide. Issues such as a slow drain, clogged gutters, a blown fuse, car trouble, yard care or a leaky roof provoked calls to Gabby's cell phone with the predictable open-liner "Do you know somebody who can...?" Moreover, independent thought or decisions by Esther were rare, even when it came to selecting a meal off a Denny's menu. Esther had to first survey what others were eating and then make a decision based on someone else's taste buds, often Gabby's. Gabby had become a surrogate husband, and the last time she checked, she hadn't asked for Esther's hand. This was not the adult relationship she signed up to have with her mother. Soon, Gabby was also playing the role of the responsible "parent" to her mother, questioning Esther's stewardship of her reduced financial resources after divorce. Gabby watched her mother shop generously and take extravagant trips, while feeling compelled to remind her to apply funds toward getting the gutters cleaned in order to protect the house from water damage. This was no-brainer priority-setting to Gabby. To Esther, it was an unnecessary bore that could certainly wait. The lighter, frivolous side of life was front and center in Esther's mind, and she needed "partners in crime" to keep the party going. When Esther's main running partner, her sister Dorothy, became involved in a serious romantic relationship, Esther's loyalties began to shift as Gabby suspected they would. Instead of happiness and support for Dorothy's developing love interest, feelings of abandonment and "hateration" of Dorothy's new-found connection bubbled up in Esther's conversation.

Shifting loyalties, self-centered interests and misplaced priorities became the norm for Esther and the headache for Gabby, who yearned to see her mother anchored with a peaceful heart, guided by her own principles and convictions instead of bending like a reed to the whims of others. "I'm afraid my mother never grew up," Gabby lamented. "She knows NOT what it means to be comfortable in her own skin."

The biblical passage from which the title of this chapter originates reads as follows: "When I was a child, I talked like a child, I thought like a child, I reasoned like a child. When I became a [woman], I put childish ways behind me" (1 Cor. 13:11). This passage has always been especially poetic to me. It's one of those scriptures that outlines one's *intended* path for growth with simple words and phrasing that convey "the obvious"—one grows up and acts accordingly. This is as obvious as curing a crack addiction by stopping the use of crack. Both *obvious* goals are simple, but not easy. Neither happens without significant effort. Many who recognize the "simplicity" of these goals will not ever be able to realize them, or at least they will require an intervention of some kind. So it is that some of us will remain forever like children in our thoughts and ways just as some of us will forever remain addicts of one kind or another. Hence, simple does not equate with easy or even desirable, the latter of which is needed for committed progression.

Related to the concept of stated desire, I am reminded of one of the three most important questions for me in the Bible, which occurs near the end of Mark 10:46-52 and again in Luke 18:35-42. The story is a common one of a blind beggar named Bartimaeus sitting by the roadside doing what beggars do—begging for money. When he was informed by the crowd around him that Jesus was passing by, he began to shout in a way that others could not ignore: "Jesus, Son of David, have mercy on me!" Others in the crowd tried to silence him, as I am sure they believed he was about to "inappropriately" ask Jesus to throw a little "cash-ola" his way. After all, having mercy on a beggar is often expressed in the form of a dollar. Jesus must have heard something different in the quality of the man's plea, as He stopped and called Bartimaeus over to Him. Now, to me, this is where the story gets interesting. You would think that, when one who needs to be healed of an *obvious* affliction meets one who has a reputation for healing that affliction, Jesus would not have to waste time with pleasantries and questions about what Bartimaeus meant by his request for mercy. It should have been quite apparent what his need was, enough to get the healing underway. However, here's the powerful question Jesus asked, one that moves me every time I read it: "What do you want me to do for you?" At face value, it seems like a silly question, but nothing could be more contrary. Jesus is *serious* about *hearing* a response from Bartimaeus because he obviously *knew* what Bartimaeus was about to say for—"Your Father knows what you need before you ask him" (Matthew 6:8). However, it wasn't until Bartimaeus answered the question in four *spoken* words, words filled with the boldness and clarity of one who is focused in his mission, that Jesus healed Bartimaeus. Bartimaeus responded, "I want to see." Notice he didn't give a lengthy response nor did he stutter, hem or haw. "Go," said Jesus. "Your faith has healed you." The passage goes on to say that, "Immediately he received his sight and followed Jesus along the road."

The conclusion of the story of the blind beggar leads you to believe that if Bartimaeus had not been *clear* in the delivery of his answer to Jesus or *desirous* of the expanded responsibilities his restored sight would bring, he may not have been healed that day. My thinking is that Jesus desired Bartimaeus to *own* his request. He wanted him to man-up and confess his vulnerability, his need, his dream, his hope. He appeared to grant Bartimaeus a gem of an opportunity to state his desire in no uncertain terms and to *go for it* as a prerequisite for receiving his healing and propulsion into a new reality. This, to me, is the defining moment, when Bartimaeus the beggar (or the child), dependent on everyone else for his survival, becomes Bartimaeus the *man* who takes initiative to put away childish things, complaints, whining and the hope that others will *guess* at his needs. He is enticed by Jesus' question to take *ownership* of his desires, and once he does so, he is freed to live a life worth living. It is a question that requires a courageous answer, because once you dare set yourself free of affliction and obstacles, you lose the ability to blame anyone else for all of life's troubles, disappointments and inconveniences. Bartimaeus now has to "see" himself into a new reality. He has to get a job; he can no longer beg on the side of the road for a living. He's lost his excuse. He now has to go get an apartment where he has to pay rent instead of living on the street for free. He's lost his excuse. Now he has to clean himself up, shower regularly and groom himself appropriately. He's lost his excuse. Now he may have to learn how to conduct himself in more intimate relationships where people actually require him to be a giver instead of just a receiver. *He's lost his excuse.* He may now need or want to go in search of a wife who may bear him children in a home where he'll be expected to be a priest, protector and provider for that household. He's lost his excuse. Being blessed of God and therefore transitioning from the child who consumes the milk to the adult who consumes the meat is not for the faint of heart. It is going to *require* an investment of time and energy. Many people may not *desire* to work that hard and rise to the occasion. They perceive the cost as just too great; life is much less complex when you are only a receiver. It is also much less stimulating, bountiful and gratifying.

I raise awareness about Jesus' question, "What do you want me to do for you?" because the answer to this question determines everything else. It is a question that forces one to articulate a possible solution, and it puts the responsibility of getting needs met and finding satisfaction squarely on the answerer. If one has no clue of what is desired from another or even what is desired of oneself, for that matter, there is NO chance of realizing steady personal growth and satisfaction in relationships. If one can organize thoughts well enough to ask the right questions of others and self, and provide brutally honest answers to questions posed, there is at least a fighting chance of having others respond in fulfilling and growth-enhancing ways.

In Esther's case, she has made a decision, consciously or not, to remain a "child" and not seek the hard answers for herself. Hence she is unanchored and her thirst is never really quenched because, similar to a hyperactive child, she is a moving target. Thrills are short-lived and focused attention is fleeting. As her protests confirmed at the beginning of this chapter, she perceives that it's just *too hard* to live life with more personal responsibility.

You may recall the concept of differentiation discussed in Chapter One. It is, in short, the process of allowing and pursuing the development of self-awareness. It is a view of self that is detached from the role others may have cast one to play in early life, while one still remains connected to intimate others without being ruled by them. It is portrayed with great humor in the movie *My Big Fat Greek Wedding*. The movie is based on a true story about the main character, Toula, mustering up the courage to go against her enmeshed, meddling, intrusive, overbearing, demanding, group-think-like family. She recasts herself as a unique individual of worth, capable of making independent, non-Greek romantic and lifestyle choices that go against her family's defined role for her in their Greek "empire." Toula succeeds, though it costs her a great deal. She has to face and overcome her fears, leave her job, redefine her loyalties, deeply disappoint her parents and dare to venture out into the "scary" non-Greek world beyond the "safety" of her parents' control and opinions. In the end, her quest for freedom obviously was a journey well worth taking even though she came to understand that her freedom was not free. It never is.

In assessing Esther's level of differentiation, we see that she was cast to play the role of the doted-upon baby girl who "shouldn't have to" do for herself and for whom a suitable caretaker or provider was always found. Unfortunately, the context of Esther's life changed and that role became obsolete faster than computer technology. Esther is the last to realize that her chosen lifestyle as a single woman *requires* something more of her. She certainly has a right to live whatever life she chooses (it's a free country as we used to say with *much attitude* when I was in elementary school). However, she doesn't have the right to hold others hostage to her whims and inconveniences, complaints and whining. These childish expressions erode the chances for mature relationships to flourish as surely as sugar dissolves in water and are indicators of the *un*differentiated life. It bears repeating that highly differentiated individuals tend to have few problems with anxiety in social situations and have more stable marriages than those who have low levels of differentiation. At lower levels of differentiation, people are *under*-responsible for themselves and/or *over*-responsible for others. These individuals are guided primarily by emotions or impulses, with little to no reliance on thought. They are generally consumed by relationships, leaving little energy for self-direction. Therefore, they tend to have more anxiety in social situations and more marital disruption than those with higher levels of differentiation (Becvar and Becvar 1996). Esther is a great example of one who never differentiated from her earliest awareness of herself as a pampered princess who was not required to think for herself or make her own way in life, and she doesn't appear desirous of doing so now. Old habits die hard. In Esther's case, growing beyond these old habits is a tall order because she side-stepped key developmental milestones. They include the experiences of friction and failure that create fortitude as we mature. Unfortunately, Gabby has had to pay the price for that, though she will not and cannot be subsumed by her mother's antics. Gabby is living a differentiated life.

Questions

1. Does my mother pull at my heart strings by trying to arouse guilt, pity or a sense of urgency in me to fulfill her needs when she is quite capable of meeting her own needs?

   _____
   _____
   _____

   What is her *modus operandi* for getting me hooked?

   _____
   _____
   _____
   _____

2. Am I left with a feeling of resentment when I once again have caved in to her intrusive and "helpless" demands? Where do I direct that resentment (e.g., excessive shopping, overeating, fights with others, choosing people for intimate relationship who are similar or the exact opposite, that is, domineering)? _____

   _____
   _____
   _____
   _____

3. What do I imagine is the worst thing that would happen if I refused to play the game anymore? What is the best thing that could happen?_____

   _____
   _____
   _____
   _____

4. How is my life being depleted by the time and energy directed toward taking care of the emotional needs of a grown, able-bodied woman of sound mind? _____

_____

_____

_____

_____

5. How would others in my life benefit if I "forced" my mother to grow up? _____

_____

_____

_____

_____

References

Bible (New International Version).

Becvar, D.S. and R.J. Becvar. 2004. *Family Therapy,* 3rd ed, 153. Needham Heights, Massachusetts: Allyn and Bacon.

CHAPTER SIX

I'm Happy for You...I Think

At age thirteen, Erica had her first undeniable epiphany that her relationship with her single mother, Hattie, was crossing that thin line between eccentric parenting and insanity. Insanity was beginning to win. Hattie, a mother who clothed, fed and educated her daughter with care had been an alcoholic all of Erica's life. In their warped dynamic, the alcoholism had become normal to Erica. It was all she ever knew of Hattie, who she had insisted on seeing as a good person and someone she needed to protect. In her eyes, Hattie had many redeeming qualities, and she was, after all, the only parent she could rely upon. However, the alcoholism, coupled with the madness that always accompanies addiction, was becoming unbearable for the young teenager. For starters, Hattie drove drunk all the time with Erica and her much older sister in tow. The small quiet voice of concern inside Erica's head was now screaming with the intensity of sirens alerting a tornado's close proximity. At first, Erica's response to Hattie's drunk driving was subtle and more subconscious; for example, she fell asleep when she rode with Hattie to avoid being traumatized by her reckless driving and near misses. One day however, this stick-your-head-in-the-sand coping skill came to an end. Erica's sleep tactic no longer overrode her increasing need for safety when Hattie was behind the wheel. It happened the week that Erica's family buried her grandmother. Anticipating that her mother would be in a drunken stupor after the funeral, Erica had enlisted her cousin for protection, saying to her, "Don't let Mom take me home…she's drunk, and she gets mean when she drinks." So when all the good-byes were said to the family and friends gathered, Hattie prepared to embark upon the long drive home. With steely resolve that defied her age, Erica felt her muscles stiffen, the expression on her face intensify and her gaze lock onto her mother's eyes with laser precision. She mustered up the courage to protest in a way she'd never done before and she voiced with unequivocal confidence, "I WILL NOT get in this car with you!" With a pounding heart, drenched palms and soaring blood pressure, Erica braced herself for retaliation, preparing to fight or take flight. She knew fighting her mother was not an option lest she be "killed," but Hattie's clenched jaw and piercing stare-downs compelled her to run for her life as though the Gestapo was chasing her. And run she did—bare feet on the unkempt urban streets of Philadelphia littered with broken glass and rusted aluminum cans, around corners and down alleyways, passing nervous and curious onlookers. While Hattie was giving threatening chase, it dawned on Erica that something was wrong with this picture. She thought to herself, in between panting and gasping for breath: "I don't know anyone else whose mother chases them in blind rages while drunk." It was a pivotal moment for Erica and for Hattie also. Afterward, the pair didn't speak to each other for two or three weeks as they each became entrenched in their stand-off, treating one another as though each was surrounded by an impenetrable force field. Eventually the situation required intervention from Erica's uncle, who soothed Hattie's rage while also summoning another relative to house Erica until cooler heads prevailed. With triumphant victory still visible on her face, Erica recalled, "That was the last time my mother drove drunk...I felt so powerful that day...I had stood up to her and it actually produced a change."

Alcohol was Hattie's self-medication for an overwhelming sense of inadequacy and a life of mediocrity, isolation and feelings of being unloved, all of which "forced" her to settle for less than she was capable of having or giving. While the alcoholism was a fierce and debilitating intrusion in Hattie and Erica's relationship, it was only one of many wrinkles that needed ironing out between them. The drinking was somewhat structured in its chaos, relative to Hattie's other vices, because the heartache that fueled it was a predictable presence. Additionally, the drinking had its own unfailing rhythm—that is, only on weekends. The more daunting issue, with unpredictable offshoots, stemmed from the shame that defined Erica's childhood because she was the product of an adulterous relationship her mother maintained for 30 years. Hattie's lover and Erica's father, Tillman, lived the life of devoted father, husband and church-goer with his "legitimate" family, who knew nothing about Erica and Hattie, and still don't to this day. Erica was never allowed to tell anyone who her father was or to relate to him *as a father* even though he visited their home three or four times a week throughout her life under Hattie's roof. She noted, "He was a frequent visitor, a 'man of God' creeping with my mother. He couldn't even tell anyone with certainty when my birthday was...we talked to each other solely through my mother." Hattie had helped Tillman, twenty-one years her senior, to keep his secrets at Erica's expense. She respected an unspoken code between them by avoiding demands on him to be a *real* father to Erica. Hattie assumed Erica was a potential source of inconvenience to him, and heaven forbid that he should be "inconvenienced" right out of her life. Instead, she settled for his financial provisions and conjugal visits while Erica settled for his cash rewards for good grades. Sadly, as Tillman's age advanced and his health deteriorated, neither Erica nor Hattie had any knowledge of Tillman's approaching last breath. Moreover, they did not have the opportunity for closure when he died as they wore "scarlet letters," which prohibited funeral attendance and therefore the opportunity to participate in shared grieving with others. No one in Tillman's circle even knew they existed.

The shame and silence of the whole sordid affair was deafening for Erica, especially because Hattie never even *attempted* to explain "the situation" to her or acknowledge the wrongfulness of this illicit affair and how it had impacted Erica's life. She left Erica to her own devices to make some sense of the situation and hold her head up in spite of it all. Hattie was accustomed to, and quite masterful at, basking in unconscious shame and isolation. Her mastery was likely grounded in her own experiences with an emotionally withdrawn alcoholic father and a mother who was the neighborhood "bookie." It stands to reason that Hattie's parents attracted some unseemly people to their home, thus exposing Hattie early in life to adult shenanigans and age-inappropriate discussions and events. While her home environment forced her to grow up too quickly, she was also the oldest girl in a family of six children and therefore expected to rear her siblings. She married at eighteen to escape so many adult responsibilities and ended up running out of the frying pan and into the fire. That "fire" was her husband, a drug addict who eventually died of a cough syrup overdose while they were separated. As if her stormy marriage was not enough to deal with, Hattie became the caretaker for her elderly father, who was estranged from her mother. Thus, the distant marriage modeled by Hattie's parents had reincarnated itself in Hattie's distant marriage to her once estranged and addicted husband. That generational history of distant marital connection didn't stop there, but was reproduced yet again in the relationship Hattie ultimately settled for with her visiting paramour, Tillman.

Despite her best efforts to make her own way in life, Hattie never found a soft place to land other than her weekend "retreats" with the bottle where she lived "in her zone" as Erica recalled. Unfortunately, this "soft place" meant that Erica's need for engagement with the outside world—Girl Scout activities, having friends over for sleepovers, visiting friends' homes—was not met. Erica's activities would have interrupted Hattie's "friendship with the bottle," as Erica described it. Hattie expected Erica to develop her own skill at living in isolation and bearing the cross of unacknowledged shame as if there was no alternative. Hattie had done it for decades. Why couldn't or shouldn't Erica? In fact, Erica did flourish as best she could, sifting out two or three high school friends whom she allowed to come to the house despite its condition. For Hattie, however, *living* life and connecting with other people was like asking Hattie to rip off her skin. Such painfully "frightening" association with others would have forced her to risk being exposed, warts and all. She would be responsible for navigating a world outside of the pseudo-safety of alcoholism and solitary confinement that only her daughters and Tillman were allowed to enter. The fear and perceived risks of the world outside of Hattie's home overrode any desire she may once have had to live a meaningful, growth-oriented, interconnected life. In her world with the bottle and her *piece* of man, she made and received few demands and was allowed to function on auto-pilot. This world seemed even tinier due to Hattie's hoarding of useless junk that made the home environment one cluttered and disorderly mass.

Hattie would never have to face her demons or reflect upon the reality of the darkness in which she lived, as long as she could limit Erica's exposure to what Hattie perceived as the "scary beyond" waiting to judge and condemn her. However, Erica rebelled against this existence and managed to thrive at school even under the pressure of her shame and forced isolation, relative to her peers' common interactions. With her sober presence and normal social skills, she inadvertently illuminated Hattie's distorted thinking and misguided path. This, in turn, may have served as the impetus for Hattie's fears and regrets, long hidden behind the bottle and reclusiveness, to surface. These closely guarded emotions eventually morphed into outright jealousy of her daughter and her developing zest for life away from Hattie's sequestered world. Erica's personal growth enticed Hattie to subtly justify her own choices by demeaning Erica's.

As Erica began to take risks that her mother had never dared to take, and it was obvious Erica's life was *not* going to be her mother's, Hattie's uneasiness multiplied, particularly when Erica became engaged. "My mother blew a gasket, vowed not to attend the ceremony and we didn't speak for three months," Erica recalled. After marrying Roderick, Erica worked hard at keeping the marriage intact through the normal vicissitudes of a young marriage. However, Erica soon noticed that Hattie was a little too quick to side with her during conflicts, as though Roderick was as unfit of a match for her as a wolf would be for a lamb. Hattie's negative sentiments toward Roderick had little supporting evidence, yet she appeared to be chomping at the bit for Erica to proclaim an end to the marriage. If she did so, it would confirm for Hattie that an attempt at legitimate marriage was really an empty and ridiculous exercise in folly. Therefore, it seemed Hattie could rationalize that *her* alternative lifestyle of longtime mistress was a better alternative to marriage. When Erica and Roderick hit a big bump in the road and separated temporarily to take a necessary time-out, Hattie was quick to chime in. "I knew he wasn't about anything when I met him…here I am having to pay the daycare for the baby…what was *he* doing?" This was a hit below the belt because Hattie had *volunteered* to help out and pay for daycare while the couple stabilized financially after purchasing a home. Now, she was throwing it in Erica's face as though Roderick was a ne'er-do-well piece of scum. When Erica reported *good* news about Roderick, Hattie's usual responses were passive-aggressive acts of war communicated by LOUD and penetrating SILENCES. Hattie's (more visible) signs of disapproval of any setback in the marriage included a curled lip or wrinkled forehead as though Hattie was boastfully saying, "I could have told you that." Her best display of active resentment occurred when she invited the now out-of-state Erica to visit her with the new baby. Hattie's invitations were laced with almost gleeful reminders that there was no room for Roderick to come as well.

Erica began to connect the dots and realized that her mother was rebelling against her being married, period. She had no words of support, encouragement or wisdom that indicated a desire to see them succeed, nor did she have a presence in their lives. Her efforts to be *nice* to Roderick were as transparent as Leona Helmsley's smile. Hence, when Erica reconciled with her husband after a six-month separation, she concluded that her mother was incapable of celebrating her marriage and its triumphs and opted to forgo telling her about their reunion. By this time she had concluded that her mother was actually jealous of her determination and marital commitment. Hattie had never persevered in marriage or in a life of growth, nor did she ever confront life's dilemmas in the way that Erica was doing victoriously. Describing her motivation for concealing the reunion from Hattie, Erica stated, "I invested myself wholeheartedly in healing my marriage. I needed to get my own head together before I could withstand whatever negative comments or innuendos my mother might throw my way." She further added, "I didn't and don't want people to think badly of my mother, but I have grown to realize that she and her life are not my burdens to carry."

Hattie's attitude toward Erica's marriage exemplifies jealousy as a state of being suspicious of a rival followed by a painful and perhaps destructive attempt to stake claims on a person's exclusive attention at all costs. It is a part of the human condition that may strike both men and women when they perceive a threat to a valued relationship by a third party, as in a new relationship or outside influences (such as Erica's husband). Jealousy is to be distinguished from appropriate boundary-setting designed to *respect* the parameters of a healthy relationship and impose an agreeable structure that *protects* it from destruction (such as a married couple might do regarding opposite-sex friendships). Jealousy is also to be distinguished from envy, which involves wanting some *thing* someone else has (*Psychology Today* 2010).

Many commonly think of jealousy as a necessary emotion that preserves social bonds. The reality is that it destroys social bonds more often than not. When a daughter achieves something in life that a mother perceives to be threatening to the preservation of her relationship with her daughter, the jealous mother is likely to be too ashamed to acknowledge her inner green-eyed monster, even to herself. Related to this, one mother was quoted in an article in *Times Online*: "I know from painful experience that even mentioning that, as a mother yourself, you might feel twinges of jealousy towards your children, is strictly taboo. The only time I confessed at a coffee morning that I'd have to swallow a big mouthful of unmaternal gall if my elder daughter succeeded in her long-term ambition to write a bestseller, the collective intake of breath from the other mothers was strong enough to suck the foam off my cappuccino." (Phillips 2007).

After all, what *good* mother doesn't want her daughter to stand on her own two feet, have happy relationships and experience opportunities that she never had? Thus, the unfathomable jealousy will be forced to manifest as "concealed" passive-aggressive jabs. Examples of these jabs, which are hard to pinpoint as the poisonous pricks they are, include subtle insults given to serve one's "best interests"; being late or dressed inappropriately for important functions; being silent when everyone else is being complimentary; obviously pouting, but saying "nothing's wrong"; "forgetting" important dates and occasions; "innocently" changing the subject or making a joke during a moment of sadness or distress; making dismissive grunts or facial expressions at good news.

The jealousy may never be articulated or fully understood even by the mother, particularly without therapy or growing self-awareness, maturity or receptivity to Godly conviction. However, the green-eyed monster will be hard to contain when it witnesses the unthinkable: a daughter forging ahead with a life that the mother suddenly realizes *she* could have had as well if she had pursued it, worked for it, overcome fear of the unfamiliar and acted with courage. Each new triumph reported by the daughter is a painful reminder of regrets, missed opportunities and time wasted on a sort of status-quo living rather than time invested in actually thriving with intention and purpose. Her daughter's achievements may sting a jealous mother like alcohol on a scraped knee as she remembers her own untreated wounds and what could have, should have, would have been if only....

Hence, a jealous mother may assault her daughter's vitality, her perseverance or her use of her gifts, because her daughter's spark may foreshadow a lessened dependence on her and incite a fear of the unknown within the jealous mom. The daughter's growing independence likely threatens the jealous mother's entire identity, which may be *defined* by her relationship with her daughter. Because of the daughter's evolution, that mother may feel that her daughter is no longer in service to her and her ideals. The mother is no longer the center of attention or someone to be idealized and placed on a pedestal, and thus may feel that the daughter is rejecting the life modeled by her.

It is important to interject that what matters most is the mother's *perception* of how her daughter treats her own personal advancement relative to her relationship with her mother, rather than the *reality* of how that advancement is *actually* treated in the relationship. In other words, the daughter could be modest about her achievements, understated in her acknowledgement of certain accomplishments or completely humbled by her accolades, and a jealous mother could still perceive her daughter as arrogant, gloating over the slightest attention drawn to her gifts and talents.

From a biblical perspective, the first book of Samuel depicts an interesting take on Saul's experience of jealousy. Saul was the first king of Israel, who rebelled against God's theocratic requirement for the office. Saul's infamous jealousy of David, his successor as chosen by God, drove him to pursue David relentlessly in an attempt to take his life. The Scripture says, "Saul was afraid of David, because the Lord was with David but had departed from Saul…In everything [David] did he had great success, because the Lord was with him. When Saul saw how successful he was, he was *afraid* of him…When Saul realized that the Lord was with David and that his daughter Michal loved David, Saul became still *more afraid* of him, and he remained his enemy the rest of his days" (1 Samuel 18:12-29, emphasis added).

The description of Saul as "afraid" and an "enemy" of David, in association with his jealousy of David, is of interest to me. It makes sense that if you fear someone, for whatever reason, you may attack him or her as an enemy in an attempt to minimize the impact of that individual over your life and your relationships. Or, you may try and browbeat them into some sort of submission so they are no longer a threat. To illustrate, imagine that an alien from space lands in your backyard. Your first reaction probably wouldn't be to approach, befriend or give the alien a basket from Welcome Wagon. You would be more inclined to attack and defend yourself because an alien's appearance would be as foreign to you as a robed Klansman at an M.L. King Day Observance, and perceived as threatening to you and yours. In a similar fashion, the loss of status or position can be frighteningly alien to one accustomed to being in charge, as was the case for Saul—who lost his kingship and favor with God—and for Hattie who lost her place as her daughter's exemplar of how life should be lived. Therefore, an attack on the one who had the *nerve* to surpass the other may be the result. When a familiar position or relationship status is lost, one must leave comfortable territory and adapt accordingly, or nurse the wounds of rejection, whether real or imagined. Some, like Hattie or Saul, have no skills in adapting or nursing emotional wounds. Consequently, as a sign of desperation, a "fear-turned-panic-turned-jealous mindset" takes over and becomes a rather transparent cover for their immaturity. As the saying goes, "Hurt people hurt people."

Saul's jealous pursuit of David offers a powerful lesson. It shows what can happen when individuals come face-to-face with what they fear in others and perceive as alien or threatening to cherished relationships and self-identity. Such encounters have the potential to produce weapons of mass "hateration," which may emerge as attempts to level the playing field by annihilating the competition to regain the attention of loved ones. Of course, instead of safeguarding the devotion of others, the opposite usually results. For instance, the oppressive tones and actions of a jealous mother may incite uneasiness within the daughter who develops a fear of sharing anything joyous. This, in turn, creates distance and estrangement rather than intimate relationship and loyal connection. However, people who love without possessiveness learn appropriate ways of nurturing and securing important relationships and have no *need* for jealousy and its related fears because as 1 John 4:18 teaches, "Perfect love drives out fear."

As Erica continues to grow and evolve, Hattie's business-as-usual style will be threatened. She'll have to decide whether to come out of her comfort zone and relate to Erica on new terms because Erica will no longer play by the same rules. In fact, having to play by new rules is exactly what created similar fears for Saul. Both he and Hattie experienced: a) fears that everyday life as previously known will be challenged and self-centered excuses will become unacceptable; b) fears that the victory of someone close to them will mean some kind of relational abandonment; and c) fears that someone with a brighter spark will unwittingly cast light on the flaws and vulnerabilities of the jealous one, who now frets about being exposed, disgraced, powerless and alone. Hattie chose to serve at the altar of her fears, possessiveness and questionable self-identity; Erica chose not to. The results speak for themselves.

Questions

1. What unachieved dreams of my mother's has she shared with me? What were the reasons she didn't attain her aspirations? _____

_____

_____

_____

_____

_____

2. Have my mother's efforts to "protect" and "shelter" me from hurt or disappointment been grounded in her actual knowledge and experience or just her own imagination?

_____

_____

_____

_____

3. How does my mother usually respond when I share good news with her about my life? _____

_____

_____

_____

_____

4. What emotions do I experience after sharing my hopes, wishes or fantasies with my mother? _____

_____

_____

_____

_____

Is there a steady rain on my parade that has become a torrential downpour? Describe a recent example. _____

_____

_____

_____

_____

5. What hurts me the most about my mother's putdowns and why? _____

_____

_____

_____

_____

6. What do I keep doing that makes me a sitting duck for her insults and injuries? _____

_____

_____

_____

_____

References

Bible (New International Version).

Phillips, C. 2007. "When the Green-Eyed Monster is Mum." *The Times*, November 24.

Psychology Today. 2010. "Jealousy." Accessed March 15. http://www.psychologytoday.com/basics/jealousy.

CHAPTER SEVEN

From Good to Grief

B EVERLY EXITED THE CHURCH ALONG with all the other well-wishers at her best friend's wedding, buoyed by the contagious happiness of the event and basking in the bridal glow she had just witnessed. She delighted in seeing two of the most deserving people she knew come together in love. She found it an especially poignant moment when the bride and groom entered their rented white Rolls Royce at the close of their reception. Beverly took the time to really absorb their grand send-off into the sunset. It was a perfectly timed moment, as though set designers had staged this backdrop for the dramatic close of a great love story. Dusk had always been her favorite part of the day anyway. It triggered reflective thoughts during her transition from work to home and also from her primary job to one of her two part-time jobs. During these transitions, she experienced a sort of existential "check-in" if you will, and she noticed that these moments were happening more frequently of late. Gnawing questions of "Who am I?" and "What is my purpose?" surfaced during this time. No answers were ever in sight these days, making the questions cry out in her mind loudly and reliably with the persistence of a five-year-old's peskiness about why the sky is blue or where does rain come from. So it was that, as she watched the bride and groom pull away, the afterglow began to fade from her spirit and was replaced by her miserable, yet familiar, companion called "Void." It stepped forward front and center with questions and reminders about her dead-end life. She became engulfed by anger and sadness, along with other emotions that were so indefinable she'd have a better chance at describing the appearance of a formless ghost. While she was happy for her friend, she couldn't help but feel the stark contrast between the progressive lives of her friends and the quicksand in which her stagnant life seemed hopelessly stuck. She felt doomed to spend the rest of her life with the daily threat of drowning in the tsunami of responsibility she had inherited by default.

You see, when Beverly's parents divorced after her nineteenth birthday, Beverly was virtually consecrated as the head of household. She became "husband" to her mother, Grace, who suffered from chronically uncontrolled diabetes brought about by habitual mismanagement of her diet. She also became "overdraft protector" for her older, spendthrift sister whose husband was frequently unemployed. When one of her sister's children had pressing needs (to which their father seemed indifferent), Beverly often loaned her credit card to her sister. With certain regularity, Beverly stood in the gap for them when there was more month than money and ends didn't meet but merely waved at each other from afar. Beverly was also the overseer concerning the needs of her schizophrenic brother who lived away from the family in a personal care home. She strived to remain in touch with him, even though it was often about as enjoyable as getting a root canal.

In short, Beverly's launch into adulthood was more of an abrupt shove off a cliff, particularly given that Grace's career ended prematurely due to her advancing diabetes. Beverly had no time to sow any wild oats. RIGHT after college, before she could smell the coffee on her first job, Grace made an executive decision to turn over the financial responsibilities of her posh, in-town condo to Beverly. Beverly succumbed to her new assignment without protest, inquiry, delay or consideration of her own best interest. The condo was unceremoniously transferred into her name with about as much forethought as one puts into swatting a gnat buzzing around one's face. When all was said and done, Beverly was obligated to pay the whopping $1,850 mortgage plus the $650 monthly association fee. Grace master-minded the plan, informed Beverly of her new-found responsibilities, and that was THAT. For a while, it worked because Beverly, still too young to fully comprehend the web in which she had been ensnared, didn't mind living with Grace. She rather enjoyed the sense of security and familiarity the arrangement offered while she stabilized as a young adult. And, as long as Beverly didn't dare make plans to grow up, leave the nest, have a life, maintain a romance, enjoy her friendships or stop buying indulgences for Grace, their relationship was "perfectly fine." It was just as perfect as Blacks and Whites in the historic South as long as Blacks didn't try to vote, use a public park for which they paid taxes, seek education or housing in segregated districts, or secure a non-servile job. In both scenarios, as long as everybody stayed in their respective pigeon holes, relationships were "just fine," weren't they?

As the compliant daughter, taught by the best of them to avoid going against the family grain, Beverly unwittingly mortgaged her future by saddling herself with the debt owed for the family's homestead, which was well beyond her means. Beverly was now full-time provider for Grace who "couldn't work"—apparently not even from home in ANY capacity. At least that's how Grace viewed it. She was still immobilized by the abandonment of her ex-husband. He paid zero alimony, remarried and turned a blind eye to Beverly's struggle to keep the boat afloat for Grace and the entire family. Beverly's complicit behavior as her mother's safety net was par for the course, and it was manifested *this time* by keeping Grace in the lifestyle to which she had grown accustomed. Notice that this is different from Grace maintaining the lifestyle for which she was *working*. Beverly did the working part, and Grace luxuriated in the fruit of Beverly's labor. Thus, Beverly was catapulted from her role as a sheltered and over-protected daughter enjoying her status as the baby of the family into the role of family nucleus upon whom everybody's survival seemed to depend. "How did that happen?" she often pondered years later. Little did she know that her thoughtless decision to passively accept responsibility for the condo had imprisoned her in a life she would one day come to loath.

Early into the new financial arrangement, Grace expressed compassion for the oppressive burdens on Beverly. She did so with the sweetness of Aunt Bee from the *Andy Griffith Show*. Soon however, that compassion gave way to a drone of complaints about Beverly's inability to make the bed with military crispness or her inability to make the grits with just the right consistency. Moreover, that original "sweetness" Grace conveyed was betrayed by the fact that she didn't lessen her demands on Beverly. Grace never wavered in her expectation that Beverly somehow muster the herculean strength required to be the overseer of...well... everything, including the acute care Grace needed after the partial amputation of a gangrenous leg. Beverly's physical availability for her mother even included the donation of a kidney to replace Grace's diabetes-damaged kidney. In every day matters, Beverly was also responsible for Grace's grocery shopping, and of course she was the financier for all household purchases "necessary" for their swank condo. Grace's not-too-subtle demands for just the right lamp for the antique mahogany console table in the foyer, or just the right silk pillow for the couch, or just the right taffeta drapes for the spring season, provoked verbal protests from Beverly for sure. However, Beverly's resistance was tempered by Grace's facial expressions when she didn't get her way, complete with puppy-dog eyes that conveyed her disappointment and pulled at the heart strings. Beverly hates seeing that face more than the pain of spending money she does not have. Though Grace's mouth says, "I understand…don't worry about getting it," her body language makes her words inaudible. It "screams" over the pseudo-sincerity of her words louder than a sonic boom.

As the good "husband" that she is, Beverly has felt herself a failure for not being able to fulfill the hopes of her "wife." Thus she is prone to caving in as quickly as a coal mine shaft, and she suffers the deadly consequences accordingly. Those consequences have been a *dying* spirit, *decaying* dreams for her future, *death* to her financial growth despite the three jobs she works, *devastating* bondage to a *depleting* relationship with Grace and *derailed* opportunities to develop relationships with peers or romantic interests. Yet Beverly perseveres through all the "husband-wife" bickering that characterizes her relationship with Grace because… well…she loves her and often feels she has no choice. Beverly has a big heart and the gift of generosity, which are currently unrestrained concerning Grace. As Beverly's "only" parent, from whom she's never lived apart except for college, Grace serves as Beverly's emotional crutch, which she thinks she needs for her own self-assurance and sense of belonging. Besides, in Beverly's childhood memories, Grace was a gifted nurturer and the rightful wearer of many a "#1 Mom" pendant. She had sheltered Beverly and her siblings through the storm of the divorce, commandeered over-the-top birthday parties, exposed the children to the arts, made herself available for their every piano or ballet recital and cheered on their educational pursuits. She was the perfect mother for little ones who depended on her for survival. However, she was unable to nurture their autonomy and the spreading of their wings they would one day need to fly away from the nest. That would have required a different goal for parenting than Grace had in mind. She was ill-equipped to love her *adult* children in this way, that is, with respect for their developing goals and interests apart from her. Even as her children grew and craved more independence from her when they were adolescents, her response was to clamp down on their outside activity. She suppressed their teenage energy and had a ready response of "no" to Beverly's requests to engage in parties, football games or dates. The message to Beverly was to stay at home; let Mama dictate what to think, what to feel and how to use her time and (one day) her money. In short, Grace's children were her LIFE, and therein was the problem. Grace had stopped developing herself long ago, including the pursuit of friendships, church family, hobbies or interests or even just comfortable solitude. The limitations she imposed on Beverly are evidence of her gripping fear at the thought of living on her own two feet, without Beverly as her primary anchor. Meanwhile, Beverly's resentment and rage grow exponentially with each passing day of "enslavement" to Grace.

How could a relationship that started out so well and filled with such joy devolve into a kinship that has Beverly mired in grief and back-breaking obligation? "I used to have my mom on a pedestal...I thought she was perfect...and now I see she isn't who I thought she was," lamented Beverly. Beverly is thirty now, and as I mentioned earlier in the book, she's reached that age when one enters the "no-spin zone" of self-awareness, that is, when scales that blind one's eyes begin to fall away. With an awakening mind and a sharpening focus, she is beginning to understand that she is not her mother, and her mother is not her. This is an important milestone to achieve in any maturing relationship. Hence, her evolving perception of Grace is becoming more reality based. Beverly now looks squarely at the human being Grace *is*. Her adult view is undistorted by her childhood perception of Grace as the all-knowing mother who had the power to heal any scraped knee, the compassion to wipe away tears after a rough day at school and the endearing ability to make the best chocolate chip cookies on the planet.

Everyone expects that one day the roles of parent and child will reverse, thus the saying, "Once an adult, twice a child." In due season parents inevitably become feeble-minded, powerless and helpless. The blessing of loving and dutiful children comes forth and the children nurture and protect the parents when they are unable to do so for themselves. This role reversal happens earlier for some and later for others. Sometimes the season of role reversal lasts for decades and sometimes just a few months, but it happens as sure as dogs bark and cats meow. In Beverly's case, it was *orchestrated* by Grace to begin the moment Beverly's father abandoned them, just as she was preparing to "soar on wings like eagles" (Isaiah 40:31) and readying to embark on a dream career in medicine.

Beverly's maturing outlook over the past decade informs her that she has outgrown the role Grace recruited and trained her to play. She is now escalating her verbal rebellion. However, for Beverly it's kind of like the mafia in that she doesn't know how to get out, nor has she fully embraced the idea that it's really possible or right to get out. She has played this role for so long, it's all she knows of her young adult life. With each passing year, she painfully takes stock of her talents, withering on the vine from inability to blossom under the weight of staggering debt and all-encompassing service to Grace and immediate family. Meanwhile, Beverly is acutely aware that Grace's health is deteriorating while her demands for living large with expensive lamps and lunches on Beverly's dime multiplies. The women of this enmeshed family, including Beverly's sister, have approached independence and autonomy with gnashing of teeth. They recoil from growth; each is embroiled in living life by default. They use each other as crutches for different reasons, and Beverly in particular expects somebody else to save them. While waiting for the rescue squad, they do not actively seek to grow beyond the vicious and repetitive cycle of debilitating debt, unemployment, illness, stress and deferred dreams. Instead, they have resigned themselves to merely surviving. They've embraced an unspoken motto of "One For All," whereby that "one" is Beverly. Notice the "All For One" part of that expression is absent because the family does not extend reciprocal support to Beverly. As the only insightful one of the bunch, Beverly is tortured by the dysfunction and lack of growth in herself and the entire family. She often questions, "Why won't somebody help me?" Unfortunately, she has yet to embrace that the "somebody" is herself.

While Beverly understands that it is Godly to honor her mother, she has no idea where honor of her mother ends and placation to a sinister force begins. Because she has been avoiding adulthood like the plague, she continues to exist in a symbiotic relationship with Grace. Their respective growth is stagnated by this bond, and they each remain trapped in a sort of perennial childhood. As Hebrews 5:13 teaches, "Anyone who lives on milk, being still an infant, is not acquainted with the teaching about righteousness. But solid food is for the mature, who by constant use have trained themselves to distinguish good from evil." Beverly and Grace are not nourishing themselves with solid food—that is, sound judgment and discernment. When there is "constant use" of such as the scripture teaches, one matures in understanding right from wrong in problem-solving and decision-making by trial and error. Otherwise, the "infant" in the adult body is prevented from developing and will continue chasing unsatisfying whims, fancies or objects of pseudo-security (like dogs chasing their tails). The resulting malnourishment and emptiness leaves one unable to distinguish good from evil. For Beverly the outcome of forfeiting her power in favor of chasing a false sense of security includes social isolation and lack of self-awareness and self-development. It also includes delayed decision-making and paralyzing fear of *acting* on her logical conclusions about the need to sell the condo. Over time, vitality has drained out of her as surely and steadily as fine sand empties from the top half of an hour glass, and Beverly is experiencing an emotional vacuum. She knows it well, but feels powerless to address it. So she continues to second-guess herself, marinating in self-doubt and endless pondering about the "right thing to do." She resists being weaned off milk and introduced to solid food. Therefore, she personifies Proverbs 27:12, which states, "The prudent see danger and take refuge, but the simple keep going and suffer for it."

Beverly has been a professed Christian most of her life, but is now as distant from God as east is from west. She finds herself too distracted by her three jobs, nerve-wrecking home life, and the overall thorniness of the path she's travelled to make time for God or to seek answers for the many questions of her faith experience. Nevertheless, she believes her current persona, including the escalating hostility in her exchanges with Grace, is a detestable and unfair representation of herself. Historically she was a nicer and happier Christian woman. She still wears a mask that conveys this to the outside world. However, when you throw the supposed "niceness" of Christendom into the equation of Beverly and Grace, the plot thickens for Beverly; at her core she desires to be a "good Christian" even though she's no longer sure what that means. She is perplexed by the question of how she can be a *nice* Christian daughter without continuing to serve her mother dutifully and enduring the resulting depletion. "Isn't that Godly sacrifice?" she wonders. How can she dishonor her mother by disobeying her wishes to be kept in this lifestyle?

In his book, *No More Christian Nice Guy* (2005), the brilliant Paul Coughlin states, "CNGs (Christian Nice Guys) pretty much believe they should just let life happen to them…Many have told me that it's far more Christian to live limply, deny your heart's desires, and keep your life in neutral because somehow, brother, this glorifies God." Coughlin goes on to posit that, "The nice often hide from life's unpleasant and disturbing messiness…their fear and inaction brings suffering to them and to those around them…they inwardly exhaust themselves in their determination to hide it [their resentment], and they are easily irritated and frustrated." Thus they dishonor the God they seek to serve.

Beverly is there, and Grace is oblivious and will likely always be. Are you a "nice" Christian daughter who has lost sight of where your mother ends and you begin? Have you chosen insufferable existence over purpose-filled thriving? Remember we weren't created to "be nice." Living in the land of *niceness* puts you in a sort of "candy land" where all the "sweet" compliance and surrender eventually make you too sick to make meaningful, empowering, constructive, life-changing contributions that define your life's calling.

Questions

1. Do I think conflict and anger are bad or are sins in and of themselves? What could be useful about conflict and anger?_____

_____

_____

_____

_____

2. Do I think that being a "nice" dutiful daughter at ALL costs is the right thing to do? What does it mean to me to honor my mother as the Bible commands?_____

_____

_____

_____

_____

3. Do I think *suffering* through the demeaning or dismissive nature of my relationship with Mama makes me more noble (as in martyr-like)? How does that make sense for my life? _____

_____

_____

_____

4. Do I think it's always selfish to have my own wants and desires for my life take precedence over my mother's? In what ways could it possibly serve others for my heart's desires to be met? _____

_____

_____

_____

5. Do I sometimes confuse serving my mother's needs with serving God's needs? How are they different? _____

_____

_____

_____

6. Do I erupt in irritable or explosive exchanges with Mama and always feel guilty that I don't have more self-control? If I were to consider that my anger and irritability originate from valid reasons, what would those reasons be? _____

_____

_____

_____

References

Bible (New International Version).

Coughlin, P. 2005. *No More Christian Nice Guy.*
Bloomington, Minnesota: Bethany House Publishers.

CHAPTER EIGHT

The Young and the Restless vs. the Old and Uptight...and the Just Plain Clueless

"NO SHE DIDN'T SAY THAT!" gasped Valencia.

"Oh yes she did, girl," grieved Michelle.

"Say it ain't so," Valencia continued through her belly aching laughs.

"I wish I could," Michelle lamented.

Those of you to whom this chapter may apply could probably fill in the blank with things your mom did or said that made you well...sort of...cringe. There is a woman I'll call Danielle, who recalled that her mother, Theodora, often confronted associates or acquaintances about their expanding waistlines with a brazen greeting of "Hey Fatso!" It is important to note that Danielle's mom was not a "slim Jim" by any stretch of the imagination, which made the greeting all-the-more remarkable; talk about the "pot calling the kettle black!" Danielle watched in horror as recipients of this dubious greeting responded with mixed expressions—shame of their new-found girth, shock at the cavalier and unexpected confrontation of it and anger about having just been insulted. Of course, Danielle's mom was **clueless** to it all and continued to converse casually as though these victims of her insensitivity *needed* her reminder that they had eaten a few too many biscuits. Theodora was also known for making odd responses to others due to her hearing impairment, which prevented her from correctly receiving others' statements. Her pride would not allow her to readily tell others about her hearing deficits, and sometimes that pride would even cause her to forego wearing the hearing aid altogether. Hence, she was likely to respond with a polite chuckle—her usual response to mask her hearing loss—if someone announced to her that a relative in the family had just *died*. Oh my! With great tightness in her chest Danielle often found herself running interference and doing damage control by interpreting for Theodora what was actually said and apologizing to the obviously bewildered. Danielle was just as much a translator for Theodora as any immigrant child would be for non-English speaking parents.

Yet another daughter, Stephanie, was still scraping egg off her face years after her mother's *faux pas*. She recalled her mother pondering out loud, during dinner one evening, to Stephanie and her new husband, as to why people were crying at their heart-stirring wedding. They couldn't possibly have been crying purely because of the sentiment that day held or the touching ceremony! She announced her conclusions to Stephanie and her husband: "I'm thinking that people were looking at you (referring to her daughter), still quite a good catch you know, and then they were looking at you (referring to her son-in-law), and they were wondering how *YOU* got *HER!*" She said this in casual conversation, out of context, without flinching or stuttering, and without any apparent regard for her son-in-law's dignity. It was as though she burped and these sooty vapors flowed out of her mouth and left smut on everybody's face at the table. She was **clueless** that she'd said anything demeaning or inappropriate to her son-in-law as she asked him to pass the bread.

One other daughter in distress, Tara, recalled a supreme example of her mother Leah's utter selfishness, which manifested itself in one command that just left Tara speechless. When a relative made an impromptu visit to the home of Tara's parents, the first thought that bolted through Leah's mind was of the scrumptious and coveted carrot cakes that she'd just taken out of the oven. "HIDE THE CAKES," went the battle-cry. "And I do mean battle-cry," Tara emphasized. Leah's directive was laced with the same commanding tone used by Chef Ramsay of *Hell's Kitchen*. "Hide the cakes, Mama?" Tara questioned with dismay. Theirs was a tiny family with enough cupboards of food to feed a whole neighborhood. "Yes, I said HIDE THE CAKES," Leah protested, providing justification of her hoarding tendencies. She explained her rationale: the cakes were… well…uh…*hers*.

Leah's candor, for lack of a better word, would have won her more gold medals than Michael Phelps if ridiculing her husband was an Olympic sport. She couldn't *wait* to share with visiting guests what a deplorable marriage she was living in (despite evidence quite to the contrary). She even became caught up in a fixed delusion that her husband, Sylvester, was intentionally leaving the door open on the mounted microwave oven so that the protruding edges would cause her a head injury. Additionally, she dreamed up ways to humiliate Sylvester and to fill Tara's ears with toxic and unfounded criticism of her father. Once she even wore a canary yellow suit to the conservative funeral service of Sylvester's brother—just for spite. She virtually burst at the seams with pride at the thought of how she was embarrassing Sylvester with her attire and refusal to sit with him, when in fact she was embarrassing herself. **Clueless.**

Then there's Ella, a mother with diarrhea of the mouth. She was an enigma to her daughter Corrine. For Ella, words just bubbled up and out whether they were grounded in evidence, knowledge, experience, facts or not. On one occasion, Ella's "victim" was a first-time care-giver named Annie. Corrine had hired Annie at an hourly rate to transport Ella, whose eyesight was failing, on various errands. Their virgin trip was to a doctor's office, which was an unusually far distance from the house. Afterwards, Annie went over her reasonable fees with Ella. *Right* out the gate, Ella unabashedly accused the good-natured Annie of padding her earnings by taking THE longest route to the doctor's office. "Hmmp, you think I don't know what you did, but I saw what you were doing…it's the oldest game in town, hmmp."

Corrine was chagrined and stunned by Ella's unexpected accusations of lying, pilfering and exploiting the elderly, and was dumbfounded by the caustic attack coming out of her mother's mouth. She had wanted so badly for this new connection to go smoothly as this was the fourth driver she'd hired, and she knew there was NO reason to believe that Annie had committed any act of deceit. With a flushed face (due to humiliation and growing rage at Ella), Corrine attempted mediation and clarification, which only fueled Ella's continued diatribe. Ella sat there proud as a peacock; she had gotten Annie *TOLD*.

Insulting care-givers wasn't the only trick Ella had up her sleeves. Ella was also known for barking orders at her family regarding their choice of restaurants; when dining out they were to exclude Japanese, Chinese, Jamaican, Italian, Mexican, Greek and family-style restaurants. She fancied herself as doing them a favor by enhancing their selectivity of "good food," as she was rife to say, and offering to pay for the meals. After outings with Corrine to a restaurant or to the hair-dresser, Ella hastened to complain about the poor quality of food or service. She usually added conspiracy theories as to how and why people were trying to intentionally sabotage her good will—she was "on to them!"

These trips often turned Corrine's attempts at a light-hearted outing into events more laborious and painful than having impacted wisdom teeth pulled. Corrine realized that Ella was, of course, **clueless.**

Last but not least is Gail. Her mother Elmyra arrived on Thanksgiving Day flustered, frantic and just plain freaking out because she forgot to bring the dinner rolls she promised to supply for the holiday feast. Gail, an attentive and dutiful daughter, attempted to soothe Elmyra and help her understand it wasn't that big of a deal, but her efforts backfired miserably. "YES IT IS A BIG DEAL," Elmyra *shouted* back within earshot of guests, using an irrationally angry tone. She continued to protest up until the before-dinner prayer, when each of the twenty or so guests was asked to verbalize one thing he or she was thankful for that year. When it was Elmyra's turn, she responded as earnestly as an innocent Catholic child giving her first confession before a priest. She stated, "I am thankful for the fact that even though my daughter does not love me, I still have my health and a full life and many who care for me…" The guests were puzzled to say the least, and Gail was left to save face with a pasted, duplicitous smile. Elmyra was simply **clueless.**

There are many reasons as to why mothers arrive or permanently reside at this place in life, where their "innocent" statements or actions throw a wet rag on a conversation or an entire social event and send their daughters searching for a hole in which to disappear. First, aging certainly brings some cognitive changes that may dull one's prohibitions "on the mouth." If dementia (formerly referred to as senility) is suspected, symptoms to watch for include: getting lost in familiar places, repetitive questioning, *odd or inappropriate behaviors,* forgetfulness of recent events, repeated falls or loss of balance, *personality changes,* decline in planning and organization, changes in diet/eating habits, changes in hygiene, increased apathy and changes in language abilities, including comprehension. However, a diagnosis of dementia may not generally be given without additional declines in social functioning and independent living (e.g., the ability to shop alone, manage finances, perform basic household duties and monitor appropriate social behaviors). Changes in social interaction may occur because of structural and neurochemical changes in the brain that affect a person's ability to process and act appropriately on information. Common functional areas affected by dementia are: a) self-awareness (reflection on one's actions and impact on others); b) other-awareness (the interpretation of another's emotions and an appropriate response); c) adherence to social norms (situation-appropriate behavior); d) interpretation of social behavior (distinguishing between what is said and what is implied); and e) interpretation of emotional cues, i.e., understanding of body language (Memory and Aging Center 2011).

Second, differences in the environmental context of the mother's rearing versus the daughter's rearing make a huge difference in how mothers and daughters come to understand each other. Between generations there are usually shifts in the norms, sometimes seismic in proportion, which create generational gaps in understanding and connection. This is where cultural tradition meets the next generation, and sparks may fly because certain traditions from "back in the day" don't always translate well in the daughter's contemporary existence. Just to be clear, I'm defining culture as something well beyond race or ethnicity. I'm referring to culture as a unique set of ingredients in which an individual marinates over the course of childhood and thereafter. This "marinade" shapes that person's worldview and perception of self in relationship to others. Ingredients could include race, ethnicity, religion or church/mosque/temple, social status, neighborhood, family heritage, friendships and a myriad of other factors. As I often say, "Where you come from casts a long shadow."

Ayaan Hirsi Ali, a Somali native and former member of the Dutch parliament, articulates these generational differences so poignantly in her book, *Infidel* (2007). In it, she described the light-years of cultural differences in the young adult lives of her grandmother, mother and herself. For starters, there was her nomadic, superstitious, Islamic grandmother who never had time to pray in the desert and never was expected to as a woman. Next was her more stationary and devout Islamic mother who was preoccupied with learning to pray properly in its purest form. She was perceived by the grandmother to be raising "worthless" children because they had the luxury of drawing water from a tap instead of hunting for it daily in the desert. The grandmother also treated the children with disdain because they had the *nerve* to live in a "cement block house with a hard roof." Ayaan then catapults from this simplistic, uneducated, hyper-religious and superstitious background to earn a master's degree on another continent, become a law-maker alongside her all-White peers and to eventually settle on an atheistic worldview. Talk about seismic shifts between the generations. She wrote, "To my grandmother, feelings were a foolish self-indulgence...I was terrified of insects, so in her eyes I was a truly stupid child...[my mother] was determined that nobody would ever have grounds to gossip that she, Asha Artan, had behaved improperly...[she] never took a taxi or a bus for fear of being seated beside a strange man." For reasons she discusses at length in her compelling book, there was little to no bridge between these generations, and the relationships deteriorated into irreconcilable estrangement.

So it is with close-minded mothers of the world, who are impacted by the generations of ancestral influence, healthy or not, in which they are steeped. These influences are sometimes barbaric acts cloaked in cultural tradition. One such example is female castration of the clitoris and sewing of one's vagina virtually shut. Many mothers allow this to be performed in North Africa, parts of the Middle East and Southeast Asia on their daughters in order to certify them as virgins and therefore marriageable (Waris 1998; Ali 2007; Wikipedia). Another cultural tradition is the breast ironing performed by Cameroon women on their daughters to keep them flat-chested and sexually unappealing to potential suitors who may rape them (Renee 2009). Both of these long-held "traditions" have now attracted international attention and will certainly be looked at with more conscious awareness and rebellion in generations to come.

Other less graphic examples of maternal guidance shaped by certain cultures might include the cultures of: a) an indulgent family or a poverty-stricken family; b) an underachieving family or an overachieving family; c) a food-centered family or a health-conscious family; d) a drug-addicted, aggressive and violent family, or a passive, non-communicative family; e) a hyper-religious family or an atheistic family; f) a family of self-centered individuals who value autonomy, or an immigrant family that values doing *everything* as one unit; g) a fanatically frugal family or a spendthrift family; h) a family victimized by racism and the sense of fear and powerlessness it incited for generations, or a family accustomed to ease, influence and privileged access to power and resources.

For instance, Leah, the cake hoarder, had been raised in an indulgent culture where she was accustomed to having her needs met *abundantly* by her mother, and where sharing with others was not a priority. Ella, who wouldn't let others in on her hearing impairment, was raised in a culture of poverty and mistrust of those outside of the self-reliant, proud family of twelve children. In their worldview, people outside of the family were not to be trusted and were considered to be potentially harmful, ALWAYS. They weren't allowed to tell anybody outside of their family, for example, that they were hungry. I suppose Ella's family feared some kind of retribution by outside authorities that could threaten the family's intact status. So, pride, dignity and self-reliance ruled the cultural climate of their home.

Whatever the case, a chasm of misunderstanding potentially awaits the mother-daughter duo. The breach will occur when the daughter is influenced by the environment of *her* day (versus the environment in which her mother was raised forty, fifty, or sixty years ago), and she begins to depart from her mother's script. One benign example of this was humorously shared by an interviewee. Her mother often chided her for chewing gum in public because in her day a "proper" young lady never did such a dastardly thing. One can only imagine the "interesting" exchanges they've had on this issue over the years. To this day, this mother has never relented.

Some mothers may be underexposed and therefore lacking in social skills and graces. The mothers who raised my generation in the '60s and '70s were often members of the first generation in their families to be college educated. They had certainly achieved a great measure of success by middle-class standards of the day. They were mostly teachers, librarians and educators in various capacities. Generally speaking, however, they were not socialized in the same way their daughters had the luxury of being. Because they were the offspring of parents whose first priority was simply survival in a terroristically racist America, they were duty and church-bound first and foremost. They didn't have girlfriends or male friends with whom they shared routine lunches or dinners nor did they talk extensively on the phone to their peers. They didn't plan fun island getaways with friends, think of travelling to exotic places or embark on career paths designed to reach ever greater heights. They didn't take clients to lunch or meet for Happy Hour after work. They worked, came home, cooked dinner and completed or oversaw evening chores in preparation to do it all over again the next day. Period. They were disciplined and orderly, and life ran like clockwork because they made sure that it did. Oh, and they NEVER mingled with, or perhaps even knew, non-Black people outside of work. These were the rules, rituals and norms that once served *them* so well in surviving their childhood and adulthood including circumstances of socio-political-racial upheaval. The mechanics of their daily lives were absolutely necessary for that season, but they've become obsolete to their daughters. Therefore, Mama may not be as socially swift as her cosmopolitan daughter who has travelled, wined, dined and interacted with people of all races and ethnic backgrounds. Thus, worlds collide because the daughter has expanded her vision of what's doable and desirable, whereas Mama may be stuck in a time warp about what's appropriate and acceptable behavior, based on an outdated context or limited exposure. Let me interject here that I am *not* referring to the timeless values and principles for living a wholesome life, such as may be found in biblical teaching, as outdated. Gratitude, humility, hard work, delayed gratification, kindness, respect for authority, saving for a rainy day and living below your means will never go out of style. Rather, I'm referring to Mama's outdated context as may be demonstrated by her discomfort in interacting with others who are different or smarter, richer or poorer or more relaxed with rules and traditions than she. Perhaps that unease may be based on certain preconceived ideas she's held for decades that "support" her insistent beliefs without the evidence of facts, personal experience or observations.

Fourth, sometimes the invincible Black mother is, believe it or not, mentally ill. This is a fact that tends to escape African Americans. By and large, African Americans tend to think of mental illness as defined by outlandish behavior that is detectable at mere glance; the inflicted will look odd and scary, have a foaming mouth and will be dragging a foot behind them as they navigate life with one eye in the middle of their foreheads. An intelligent client of mine once described her mother's "personality" as textbook psychosis (characterized by a fixation on bizarre delusional thoughts, just to name one hallmark symptom). Her mother poured bleach on everything in her car, office and home, and ruined couches, car upholstery and the like because she was convinced she was under attack by insidious germs. When I suggested that her mother was suffering from mental illness and in need of professional help, my client was aghast as though I had spoken blasphemy. The thought had never even crossed her mind. So it goes in the Black community oftentimes when it comes to mental illness. These types of episodes go untreated and are tolerated by a shared understanding amongst family members: "That's just how Mama is."

Fifth, the bitter taste of successive disappointing experiences can cause someone to feel as if they are wearing dark sunglasses in a museum of the world's greatest and most vibrant fine art collection. The vibrancy of a Henri Matisse painting would be dulled when viewed through dark sunglasses, which are designed to filter out the brilliance of what passes through their lens. So it may be with the occurrence of one more dashed dream, one more "life-comes-at-you-fast" event, one more family disaster, one more act of negligence, one more health crisis or one more missed opportunity. All these examples have the potential to tip the proverbial apple cart in the direction of a selfish, super-sensitive, suspicious or sullying response style without conscious awareness. As Proverbs 14:10 teaches, "Each heart knows its own bitterness."

Naomi from the Book of Ruth comes to mind as an example of how bitterness can consume one after one too many hardships (1:1-22). After a series of tragic losses, Naomi is seen focusing on the negative (understandably) in everyday conversation in ways that are out of context. Naomi was the wife of a man named Elimelech who died. Later her two adult sons died as well. In addition to the emotional impact of these losses, Naomi lost her sources of financial support. It was culturally taboo—if not impossible—for a woman of her day to make her own living. By the way, these tragic deaths occurred after the family had already endured a famine in the land, the apparent driving force behind a move from Judah to a foreign land. After the deaths of her sons, she decided to move yet again back to her hometown of Bethlehem. So in summary, that was a famine, three deaths of immediate family members and two moves under Naomi's belt. Any ONE of these tragedies would have been debilitating enough, let alone all of them occurring in a relatively brief span of time (though the Bible doesn't say exactly how long). To say that Naomi had experienced her fair share of bitter heartache is an understatement. She responded initially by trying to isolate herself from her only intimate family connection, her two daughters-in-law with whom she was very close. Naomi nudged them to leave her, return to their mothers and find husbands with whom to have children as she stated of herself, "The Lord's hand has turned against me!" (1:13). Pushing away the *only* semblance of help she was likely to have was not the most rational idea during such a time of uncertainty and with a distressing future on the horizon. One could argue that she was either totally selfless in thinking about the needs of her daughters-in-law *or* reacting from a place of irrational bitterness. Her subsequent actions lead me to the latter explanation. Whatever the case, and whether or not Naomi was just blowing smoke, one daughter-in-law took her up on the offer. She kissed Naomi good-bye and went back to her homeland. The other one, Ruth, proved to be extraordinarily loyal and was determined to go with her. Finally Naomi had to stop urging her to leave. When the two women arrived back in Bethlehem, Naomi would not even allow herself to be properly greeted by a community who hadn't seen her in many years—maybe even decades. As the townspeople attempted to re-connect with her, she shut them down by saying, "Don't call me Naomi...call me Mara [which means bitter], because the Almighty has made my life very bitter. I went away full, but the Lord has brought me back empty. Why call me Naomi? The Lord has afflicted me; the Almighty has brought misfortune upon me" (1:20-21). Imagine *that* as a response to the welcoming and curious hometown folks. Naomi quickly extinguished any flicker of excitement over her return and any joyful exchange.

Fortunately, there is a happy ending to the story as Naomi's loyal daughter-in-law Ruth went on to marry a rich and compassionate relative of Naomi's, Boaz, who sired a child with Ruth. That child was the grandfather of David, the great king of Israel and the forefather of Jesus. Naomi's bitter experiences had not been in vain after all, and there was Godly purpose in her suffering that leaves Naomi with a sense that it had all been worth it. Her one loyal daughter-in-law is said to have been "better than seven sons" (4:15). The book ends with Naomi holding her newborn "grandchild" and appearing restored in her ability, it seems, to savor a renewal of hope for a brighter future.

Working toward a "*happy* ending" for you and your mother may not be possible depending on the circumstances. At the least, I urge you to begin thinking in terms of a peaceful ending with her, perhaps from a distance, as you start by asking yourself these questions.

Questions

1. In consideration of some reasons listed in this chapter, what are some possible and reasonable explanations for my mother's odd behavior?_____

_____

_____

_____

_____

2. What are the circumstances of my mother's early life experience that I may not have factored into the equation of her behavior and our relationship? _____

_____

_____

_____

3. Have I assumed my mother ought to know better when in fact she may not? Give an example._____

_____

_____

_____

_____

4. What do I continue to expect of my mother that she is incapable of giving me? _____

_____

_____

_____

_____

5. Am I really expecting my mother to suddenly change her ways? _____

_____

Is it time to embrace acceptance of her as she is, versus trying to mold her into who I hope she'll eventually be?

_____

_____

_____

_____

6. Are there some medical or psychological issues that I've been in denial about addressing that I need to act on? If so, what step can I take tomorrow to get her the professional help she may need? _____

_____

_____

_____

_____

References

Ali, A. 2007. *Infidel*. New York, New York: Free Press.

Bible (New International Version).

Memory and Aging Center, University of California, San Francisco. 2011. "Social Skills." Accessed March 15. http://memory.ucsf.edu/brain/behavior/social.

Renee, D. 2009. "Breast Ironing of Young Girls in Cameroon." http://www.youtube.com.

Waris, D. and C. Miller. 1998. *Desert Flower*. New York: Harper Collins

Wikipedia. 2010. "Female Genital Cutting." Accessed December 7. http://en.wikipedia.org/wiki/Female_genital_cutting.

CHAPTER NINE

Now What?
(The Eight Don'ts)

Blessed Are The Peace*makers*...Matthew 5:9

ALL OF THE VIGNETTES PRESENTED in this book are true stories though names and minor details have been altered to protect the privacy of those who eagerly shared their stories with me. You have taken a quasi-panoramic tour through a handful of challenging mother-daughter relationships. Each daughter has an enduring love for, and connection to, her mother despite Mama's antics. Their stories represent a small sampling of mother-daughter issues and the daily toll of these dyads. I've concluded that, from the perspective of the adult daughters, the common thread is the tension, strain, anxiety or hostility in the relationship emanating from the mother's resistance or refusal to continue growing emotionally, experientially, mentally or spiritually (excluding cases of mental illness or cognitive decline). In other words, the mothers have had little to no life apart from their daughters, and as the saying goes, "If you're not growing, you're dying." The thing about decay is that it affects or destroys whatever is around it. All the mothers, for different reasons, are stuck in some way. That stunted interpersonal development manifests itself in a cornucopia of quirky response styles that chip away at the healthy aspects of their relationships with their daughters. Thus, I have concluded that the best way for a mother to love her adult daughter is to continue developing her *own* life, shunning any temptation to make an idol of her daughter and be totally consumed with her affairs That includes the pursuit of good health along with enriching and stimulating experiences that may not include the daughter at all, and certainly do not *depend* on her as the sole engine for Mom's mental and physical health, sustenance and growth. In this way, the daughter is unburdened to soar without guilt, worry or futile attempts to live Mama's life for her.

The good news of this book is that each of the daughters featured has decided that the buck will stop with her; the arrested development and dysfunction of their mothers will not be visited upon the next generation. They have sought intervention to empower them to do so, and that same opportunity exists for you.

The book has included mothers who worry, drain, criticize, control, envy, manipulate and/or embarrass their daughters ad nauseam. Yet, in each case, these relationships are surviving—albeit with gnashing of teeth at times, shifting loyalties and restructured boundaries along with new coping strategies. Nevertheless, they are intact relationships where there is frequent, if not daily, contact in spite of the differences and conflicts. Some daughters are limping along in the relationship, battle-scarred and weary from the journey. Others are feeling every passing moment of the relationship with an excruciating crawling of flesh akin to what one feels at the sound of fingernails scratching on a blackboard. Some have reached a fairly transcendent place wherein they've developed Teflon skin so that most of Mama's annoyances can't stick. How does this last group reach such a transcendent place? I'm glad you asked.

First and foremost, please don't forget to start with prayer. I'm not even counting this as one of the following "don'ts" because it is so essential. It deserves to be an indispensable foundation for all of the rest of my suggestions. Please understand that you *weren't* designed to maneuver difficult relationships of any kind using just your own strength, least of all those that cause the hair on the back of your neck to rise. Thankfully, we can glean from the Book of Job that no circumstance befalls the one who is surrendered to God without first going through God's loving filter. So, if you're in an uphill battle in your relationship with Mom, be of good courage and fear *not* because it comes as no surprise to God. He knew these days would come upon you long before you were in your mother's womb (Jeremiah 1:5). As the "inventor" of the mother-daughter relationship, God knows the pitfalls and snares that have caused you to stumble and that await you in the future. So save yourself some precious time and energy, and PLEASE invite His expertise into the equation with a prayer that may sound something like this:

> Father God, you see the strain in my relationship with my mother, and you know better than I ever could what's at the heart of the distress. I thank you that I can count on you to strengthen me in my walk through this as I deepen my trust in you and my belief that you are God almighty—all by yourself—and that you know what you're doing. You have a plan and purpose for my good and not my destruction. Therefore, invade this relationship and lead us out of these dark days and into your marvelous light as you guard my heart from hurt, disappointment, misunderstanding and dismissiveness, teaching me to endure to the end and stretching me in the process.

I will get out of your way and give you my mother
for you to have your way over her life and for you to
order our words, behavior, comings and goings as you
see fit. Holy Spirit, empower me to set appropriate
boundaries and to release my vision or fantasy of what
I'd like this relationship to be in favor of discerning
how best to handle the relationship as it actually is
today. Grant me guilt-free conviction to run the race
you and only you have set before me…in the name
of Jesus, Amen.

So many times we pray for the co-worker facing surgery or
the lady at church who lost her job, but we may forget to take
ourselves or those closest to us into *serious* prayer. I am a big fan
of forty-day prayer vigils with a prayer partner(s). This kind of
steadfast prayer in partnership fosters greater accountability and
enriched prayer experiences when there are issues of particular importance or burden. Try it, as it relates to your mother,
and journal how your heart changes toward her and grows in
liberation of whatever bondage the relationship has entrapped
you—even if the *circumstances* don't change immediately. The
important thing is that *your perspective* will readjust, helping you
to create a refreshingly "new normal" in your mother-daughter
interactions. Will you still have bad moments, days, weeks and
months? Yes. Will your mother-daughter odyssey be peppered
with tearful setbacks, explosive outbursts of anger or mind-
blowing dismay from time to time? Maybe. But that's okay.
The *totality* of what you feel and how you behave "in spite of"
will be remarkably less emotional and more transcendent. You
will taste, therefore, how God has done His work in you while
you persevere one day at a time. You will marvel at the gifts of
tolerance, patience and self-respect *post-prayer* versus the vulnerability to emotional collapse or derailment you experienced
three weeks ago, three months ago or three years ago *pre-prayer*.

Now, you may be saying, "If one more person tells me to pray about this I'll barf." I feel ya, which is why I'm not asking you to just "leave this at the altar" as we so often say in the church community. Rather, I'm asking you to start there *AND* continue there while you increase your self-awareness and prepare to take *action* in the here and now. I'm a practical kind of gal, so here are some of my suggested strategies and perspectives to live by:

1. Don't Get in the Ring with Mike Tyson Unprepared

Understand that your mother is quite masterful at whatever defense or coping mechanism she's developed over the years. Her style has been decades in the making, and she's been honing and perfecting her skills since well before you were even a thought. Therefore, two precautions come to mind:

a) Forgo the unrelenting need to argue your case with her when in fact she's NEVER "gotten" your perspective before and, short of a burning bush experience, may never "get it." Insanity is humorously defined as doing the same things over and over, and expecting different results. Therefore, it is "insane" and a waste of breath to keep protesting and pleading with someone who isn't interested in your rationale and has never shown any evidence of such. Like someone who brings a knife to a gun fight, you will be no match for her expert defensive skills. So save your breath and let either your silence be your response (because silence does indeed speak volumes) or let your actions or inactions do the talking for you. For example, leave the room, change the subject or do what you had planned to do anyway without seeking her permission or approval. Set yourself free!

b) If you're attempting to reconcile with your mother over some long-ago injury that left an undeniable black eye on the relationship, please take heed. DO NOT pour your soul out to her about your hurts and disappointments **IF** you are not prepared for her to respond by throwing a box of Morton's salt on the wound. "I'm sorry you got your little feelings hurt. I did the best I could. How could you say that after all I did for you? What about all the times you hurt *me?*" These might be the types of responses you'll receive. **OR** she may fall silent on you and pout, and fail to acknowledge your emotional injuries. Whatever the case, bring into focus with magnifying-glass clarity why you want to approach her and what you hope to accomplish. If you haven't done the work of a maturing heart (through prayer, therapy, journaling or counsel from others who've been there), then don't go there *at all*. If your mother appears to have had no such intervention in *her* life, *expect* a defensive response because time *alone* does not heal old wounds and personality clashes.

Your steadfast belief that the benefit of freeing your soul and making a proactive *attempt* to address the proverbial elephant in the room may be compelling enough to take the risk of confronting her about the past. In this case, give it a whirl, but proceed with caution. I wouldn't advise going there without asking the Holy Spirit to prepare your heart and hers with fertile ground. In so doing, you have a better chance of planting a seed or maintaining your composure by resisting a retaliatory response laced with rancid anger. You may be able to defuse a potentially explosive exchange by calmly responding, with good eye contact, to a "jab" thrown your way with something such as, "I choose to forgive you for that. Do know that I came in peace and will leave this discussion in peace. I wanted to begin the process of making things right with us today, and I see that's not possible at this time. You now have information about how I feel, and what this relationship needs for us to grow closer. Do what you will with that information, as I leave you to God. Be blessed." Then SHUT UP and exit—not in a huffy blaze of glory, but with the fruit of the Spirit, namely love, peace and self-control, because a "gentle answer turns away wrath but a harsh word stirs up anger" (Proverbs 15:1). You won't be able to do that in your own strength, just as you'd never expect to get in the ring with Mike Tyson and be victorious in just your own strength. You'd need a miraculous intervention to penetrate a "Mike Tyson," and that's what God provides. Take heed to 2 Corinthians 12:9, which describes God's counsel to the apostle Paul: "My grace is sufficient for you, for my power is made perfect in weakness." The commentary for this passage in the New International Version goes on to state, "Human weakness provides the ideal opportunity for the display of divine power."

2. Don't Use These Four Words

For prickly discussions such as those described in the previous strategy, let me offer this short and simple advice that works wonders in avoiding pitfalls and landmines. It is quite common advice in self-help circles. Take the words "never," "always," "ought" and "should" out of all potentially heated discussions with your mom, or with anybody else for that matter. When trying to have discussions with her on sensitive topics that could be explosive, the use of these four absolute, or blaming words, is akin to throwing gasoline on a smoldering fire. Their inclusion is almost guaranteed to turn a heated discussion into a full-blown inferno. You might be tempted to say something such as, "You never supported me," or "You always catered to my sister as your first priority," or "You always expected me to fail," or "You never remember the positive things I did." Perhaps you find yourself saying, "You should have known better," or "You ought to take a look at yourself." In the best-case scenario, these words distract from the heart of the discussion because people feel the need to stop and defend themselves or correct whether something is "always" or "never" true. Hence, the original point is lost in the shuffle. In the worst-case scenario, old wounds are reopened as new weapons are discharged under the perceived threat of misleading, shaming or exaggerated accusations. Therefore, choose less arousing descriptors to describe behavior, such as "usually," "seldom," "rarely," "oftentimes," "more often than not." Also, consider using phrasing such as, "I needed you to…" or "I missed having your attention…" or "Please try seeing it from my persective…" to replace the "shoulds" and "oughts." These are easier to digest and less likely to implode your discussions.

3. Don't Be Surprised When…

…Mom tries to pull you back into conforming to her ways. Those who may abuse the privileges of being in relationship with you are *never* happy with the fact that you're no longer available to serve their needs at the expense of your own. So Mom may make statements with disapproving tones such as "You've changed…what happened to you?" Don't fret or be deterred. That's supposed to happen! When you change, others are forced to change in response to you. And that's a good thing, even if it doesn't feel so good at first. Expect discomfort initially, but be patient with yourself and your mom as you both adjust to the new assertive you. Your goal in becoming assertive isn't to seek your mom's agreement on every point of view but rather to enhance opportunities for a deeply loving relationship that allows for respect of yourself as well as Mom *and* the inherent differences.

If Mom *insists* on conjuring up the "old you" like a sorcerer calls up the spirits of the dead, you may need to put some distance in the relationship while you grow stronger. You may create some distance by increasing delays in returning her phone calls, peacefully resisting response to any of her detracting comments or purposefully changing the subject when she begins to rain on your parade. She'll notice that you're no longer responding and will realize her diminishing influence in halting your expanding horizons. You may advance her understanding of the relationship's changing dynamics by saying something such as, "I appreciate you caring enough to notice that I've changed. It's unfortunate that you're uncomfortable with my growth right now, and I hope we will all adjust in the not-too-distant future.

I'm here to love and honor you, and I would love for us to grow in our understanding of one another as adult women. So let's be patient with each other and celebrate what we have in common."

When feeling guilty about your changing interactions and tempted to return to your old ways, try on a quote from Maya Angelou as a personal mantra that may keep your new-found mission moving forward: "I did what I knew how to do at the time. When I knew better, I did better."

4. Don't Use Mom As an Excuse for Poor Stewardship

Piggy-backing on the prior strategy, it bears repeating that Mom is not going to like it when you change the rules, especially when it comes to financial accommodations. If your mother has treated you more like a bank or loan officer, do know that mismanagement of your financial blessings or going into debt to satisfy the whims of a demanding mother is not what the Bible had in mind when it commands us to honor our mothers. If Mom is elderly or infirmed in some way, investigate all possible options for quality, safe and affordable choices for her care, clothing and feeding. These options may or may not be ultimate *preferences* for her. Likely it will be impossible to provide her with a life that perfectly suits her as she ages, regardless of how hard you try, because it won't be the life *she* created, about which she may still fantasize. However, remember that honoring Mom does not mean inviting bankruptcy into your life. She can never have enough of what she didn't need in the first place, so abandon the guilt and do what you can to secure her needs and some of her wants without ever enabling her to be a squanderer of YOUR resources. It will likely breed unnecessary resentment and anger in you if you don't. Therefore, guard against potential ill-feelings by choosing longevity and long-term peace in the relationship. You can achieve this by setting appropriate boundaries that protect you from being financially indebted or depleted. One great resource for setting healthy financial boundaries in general is Dave Ramsey and his Financial Peace University classes offered all over the country and online. To put you on the road to mature stewardship—even when it comes to Mom—try finding his radio broadcast in your area, visiting his website, www.daveramsey.com, or reading any of his books.

5. Don't Ever Think It Makes Sense to Debate With A Brick Wall

If Mom persists in provoking you into seeing or doing things her way, stop verbalizing your response. Let your *actions* speak louder than words, and give her the freedom to assume responsibility for her choices. Know that she probably won't like this because responsibility feels scary to those who would rather scapegoat someone else for mishaps and setbacks rather than face the person in the mirror. One of my interviewees for this book told me a hilarious story of how her mother protested an upcoming family trip to celebrate a relative's fiftieth birthday party. Her mother felt that the event's planners had not paid her enough homage in terms of bending over backwards to encourage and welcome her attendance. The mother protested for weeks as plans drew near, repeating with parrot-like quality, "I don't know if I'm going." Even after the airline tickets were purchased, she persevered, "I don't know if I'm going." As they drove to the airport and exited the car for the soon-to-depart flight her mother was ridiculously still protesting, "I don't know if I'm going." Finally, my interviewee and her husband declared matter-of-factly in the airport parking lot, "Fine. Catch a cab home. We'll see you when we get back." Of course, this is not the response this mother wanted because now she was being held accountable for her own statements and choices.

Needless to say, the mother caught the plane and went to the party. However, she gave her daughter the silent treatment the whole day and night because her game of "pay me some attention and cave into my rebel-without-a-cause mindset" had unexpectedly ended when her bluff was called. By the way, her pout stopped no one from having a good time at the party.

The point is that there is much freedom to be gained when you *embrace* your mother's choices and her style of operating as *her own* and forgo the temptation to coerce her into a "more appropriate" decision or way of life. As you become more accepting of her choices, making room for her *modus operandi* (however odd or unreasonable so long as it doesn't endanger her or leave her vulnerable to predators), you also hold her *responsible* for the consequences of those choices. She may then become more accepting of *your* input or *your* choices because she would have experienced the "freedom-to-choose" mindset modeled by you. You may have to bite your lip initially as you will want so badly to volunteer your opinion, your counsel, your better judgment, your protection, your quicker and better way of doing things. Ironically that's likely the same thing that annoys you about her—her intrusiveness where she is not invited.

Keep in mind that there's always a delicate balance between control and autonomy in any committed relationship, that is, a certain amount of firmness and structure balanced against freedom (or at least some wiggle room). As famed psychologist Dr. Marsha Linehan asserts in her voluminous body of work on dialectical behavioral therapy (DBT), change can be promoted by pushing acceptance, and acceptance promoted by pushing change (Shearin and Linehan 1994). In other words, the closer you move to joining with your mother by embracing *her* perspective (i.e., acceptance), you may be shocked to discover that she moves closer to *your* starting position (i.e., changes her stance in your favor). The room she then makes for your perspective (a change from the normal state of locked horns) in turn promotes greater mutual acceptance in the relationship. For example, imagine the case of a mother working well past her retirement when it's apparent to everyone else that her health and peace of mind would benefit if she retired and took it easy. The more others attempt to *control* her by pushing for her to reduce her stress through retirement, the more she may dig in her heels with a decision to continue working. However, a different result may occur if a wise daughter, for instance, decides to honor her mother's wishes by *accepting* her desire to keep working regardless of her thoughts that the mother should retire. The daughter does this by releasing *her* agenda and verbalizing to her mother with sincerity (not manipulation), "You're not ready, and I respect that you have earned the right to retire when you're good and ready." In hearing this, the mother may feel quite relieved of the pressure to conform and may relinquish the fight to protect her independence (because there's been a *change* in the expected battle of the wills). Now that she has no need to save face and defend her pride, she is free to lower her defenses (since no more arrows are coming her way). She may end up being more *accepting* of the daughter's original position to go ahead and retire. Consequently, each of them feels more pleased with the outcome. They also have the opportunity to experience greater acceptance in their relationship because the mother was given the choice to make the decision herself versus having a decision imposed upon her. It's a free country after all.

6. Don't Leave Home Without It

Always keep one essential tool handy and accessible: the word "no." This lovely two-letter noun doesn't have to be delivered with meanness or accompanied by a lengthy justification of its use. If you respond with lengthy explanations before you finally get "no" out of your mouth, you then embody the famous quote from Shakespeare's Hamlet, "The lady doth protest too much, methinks," meaning you leave people suspicious about the integrity and firmness of your response. It's actually possible to say no, politely of course, and let it just ring in the air as its own sentence. It's a liberating word that indicates you have pondered certain consequences in your mind and concluded that something's not right for *you*. There's no need to provide a dissertation to support your conclusions, with "reasons" that sound something like, "Well I would do it if I could but I have to go get my car out of the shop and then I have to go grocery shopping and then I have to churn butter, milk the cow and put a new roof on the house." These explanations tend to go from the feasible to the ridiculous. Instead, you simply say something like, "No, I'm not able to but thanks," or, "No, not this time; I have other plans," or "No, I'll pass on that but maybe next time," or a real simple but polite, "No." And then SHUT UP! Oh what FREEDOM!

By the way, when not sure of what response you'd like to give, buy yourself some time by simply sleeping on it and saying something like, "Let me think about it and I'll get back with you tomorrow." Most responses are not required right away. The next day you will have better perspective and an opportunity to give a more thoughtful, non-flustered answer rather than a rash one that saddles you with a commitment to your mother born out of a need to be a people pleaser. As Proverbs 29:20 teaches, "Do you see a man who speaks in haste? There is more hope for a fool than for him." Taking the time to think about your responses is not a passive retreat but rather a wise, purposeful act of self-control and assertion that safeguards against suffering in silence. Also, it keeps you from having to *undo* commitments made in haste. An overcommitted life or commitments to events and circumstances that do not reflect your true self may fool you into thinking you're living a full, emboldened life. The quick, but inauthentic "yes" to Mom will relieve pressure in the short term and keep the peace but will provoke anger and irritability with self and Mom in the long run. Therefore, go for long-term contentment in your relationship with Mom by simply [letting] your "yes be yes and your no, no." (Matthew 5:37).

7. Don't Expect an Elephant to Meow

"Radical Acceptance" is a phrase coined by the previously mentioned Marsha Linehan, PhD, which simply means accepting the unacceptable and finding your peace accordingly. That is, you embrace the reality of *what is* rather than the fantasy of *how you'd like things to be*. In the process, you find a cure for misery. You may have to radically accept that your mom is one of those people with whom you *have* to interact and who will not be moved by any amount of assertiveness, politeness, kindness, service, admiration or deference. There may be nothing that will win her over to a more mature, loving, compatible, less complaining relationship with you. As unfortunate as it is, accept that she may continue to bully, demean or dismiss your needs, which really tells you more about *her* state of mind (e.g., unhappiness, loneliness, bitterness) versus anything about your worthiness. Know that these types of people exist and you'll never be able to fix or heal them. That is a God-sized assignment, so scratch any prolonged concerns about her brand of drama off your list of things to *worry* about. You will be liberated from the incessant need to try harder to earn her respect, acceptance, love, appreciation, understanding, support, apologies or acknowledgement of your accomplishments—to no avail—and from wasting precious time wondering what's wrong with you. You may want to adopt a self-talk reminder for yourself that will bring you back down to normal when you start to feel your blood pressure rise. Whenever I encounter these difficult types of people, I am able to stay out of the fray *most of the time* by reminding myself of a highly sophisticated clinical intervention and complex ideology: "She just AIN'T ABLE!" Just as you wouldn't expect an elephant to meow or a cat to bark, don't expect your mother to behave out of character for her. When she tap dances on your "reserve nerve" as a friend of mine often says, understand that she is likely "characteristically in character."

Radically accepting your mother, warts and all, does not mean you *like* what she does any more than you *like* getting a wisdom tooth pulled. However, in order to heal your toothache, you had to radically accept that: a) the tooth pain was real;

b) your inflamed gum was an ugly site; and c) the pain was not going away no matter how much Advil you ingested or warm saltwater you swished around in your mouth. The acceptance of that pain's reality became the impetus for action and change (i.e., finding a *lasting* solution with professional guidance and getting the tooth pulled). Hence, radical acceptance means you refuse to be stymied by the pain or uphill battle any longer. You forgo the temptation to derail your momentum by thinking that this day, this time, this exchange, this Band-Aid solution will somehow yield the desired result without some kind of new intervention on your part. That new intervention could be tangible or intangible. It could be bold action that disrupts business as usual, OR it could be a quiet or even silent resolve to redirect your energy and concerns toward matters where you enjoy greater impact, encouragement or control. In either strategy, you liberate yourself to get on with the business of living an abundant life in spite of distractions or roadblocks from Mama.

8. Don't Go It Alone

While this book may be helpful in jump-starting your journey to wholeness in relation to your mother, it is not a replacement for therapy, which you may need to investigate. It is my hope that the book will help clarify your thinking, increase your self-awareness and help you understand that you're not alone. You may come to therapy thinking the problem is how to change your mother. Instead, you may discover that the problem is really: a) your inability to set boundaries with anyone; b) your inability to stand on your convictions; c) your feelings of inadequacy when you're around Mom or any authority figure; d) your continued emotional dependency on your mother stemming from an undeveloped life; or e) your misguided thoughts about your obligation to exhaust and deplete yourself for her as the "right" thing to do. Whatever the case, I encourage you to enlist the support of a good therapist. I suggest you call 1-800-New-Life to find one near you. Don't let another day go by without taking some action to bring a healthy intervention into your struggles with Mom. The longer you wait, the more opportunities grow for resentment to build.

References

Bible (New International Version).

Shearin, E.N. and M.M. Linehan. 1994. "Dialectical behavior therapy for borderline personality disorder: Theoretical and empirical foundations." *Acta Psychiatrica Scandinavica*, 89 (379, Suppl): 61-68.

CHAPTER TEN

Don't Stop Now: What Else? (The Eight Dos)

JUST IN CASE I DID not yet touch on a particular issue or a strategy that speaks to your situation, here are eight more suggestions for *making* genuine peace rather than *keeping* a false peace with Mama. Read on and continue learning how to recognize, confront and overcome your strained relationship with Mom in these next eight strategies.

1. Do Understand That You're Not Your Mom and Your Mom Is Not You

Before you poo-poo the headline above, know that this is not as simplistic as it appears. I was recently in conversation with a fifty-year-old woman who was *aching* to leave the church of her childhood in search of a more suitable spiritual home for herself. However, she was absolutely paralyzed to do so because "[her] mother would die." I know of another woman in her sixties who is still coming to terms with the irreplaceable quality time she lost with her children in favor of honoring her deceased mother's excessive commitment to household chores and over-the-top cleaning rituals. So you can easily see that for some good and grown women, separating from the ideals of Mama is, in fact, a *huge* milestone in thinking.

If you're finding *your* ways, likes, dislikes, vision for your life, ideals about marriage, family and parenting to be different from your mother's in some ways, congratulations! You are a uniquely designed image of an infinitely creative God who equipped you for His purpose and not your mother's. Take heart, fasten your seatbelt and prepare to enter womanhood guiltlessly and assuredly though you may be decades beyond the legal adult age of eighteen. Know that seeing your mom as an individual, a flawed human being like any other human being on the planet—not designed for carbon copying—is a sign of your maturity. IF you allow it, this honest look at Mom may also expand your acceptance of your own flaws and your expectations of others. When you consider how capable you are of messing up life with shortcomings, various inadequacies or self-centeredness, your awareness of *needing* God increases. By doing so you make room for more in-depth reverence for Him, the one who actually does call us to be transformed in the image and likeness of *Him*. "Be imitators of God...," states Ephesians 5:1. It doesn't say, "Be imitators of Mom." Anyone who distracts you from His blueprint for your life needs to be dethroned from the pedestal if you want life to flourish with divine-right success.

Therefore, engage in brutal honesty with yourself and take stock of the decisions you've been making. That would include a review of the lifestyle you've been living, the choices you've been discarding, the expectations you've carried into marriage, the career track you've pursued, the parenting style you've adopted—mainly because they were your mother's ideas or maybe even a defiant rebellion against her ideas that still betrayed *your* truth. They may have been good ideas for sure, but were they God-ideas? I suggest you journal your thoughts on this matter, getting them out of your head and on to paper where the intangible reality of your thoughts becomes seeable, "organizable," containable, correctable and manageable. As you decipher the source of your thoughts about life and its purpose, be brutally honest about what's driving you to feel out of sorts and to make choices that leave you feeling discontent or uncertain of your steps. As you do this, allow the wisdom of Proverbs 23:7 (KJV) to help you connect the dots of your life: "For as he thinketh in his heart, so is he…"

2. Do Teach Her How to Love You As an Adult

I once had a client who was married to a man who had come from a harsh background where he had never experienced loving instruction or concern. There were two emotions expressed in his family: anger and its close cousin rage. Consequently, in marriage, he had a limited repertoire of feelings from which to formulate his responses. When communicating with his wife, he copied his family's combative style of communication regardless of the context. On one occasion, she was pulled over by the police for driving too fast and was given a warning instead of a ticket. After the police left, her husband proceeded to lambast her for being so careless and for driving so inattentively. He shouted and huffed and puffed until he had veins popping out of his neck as he chastised his smart, beautiful wife in the same fashion as a drill sergeant. My client, quite an emotionally mature and insightful woman, had nothing left to give to his characteristic rants after years of these types of exchanges. She stated with impressive composure, "I think what you're trying to tell me is that it scares you when I drive too fast, and you're concerned about the safety of me and our daughter." Her composure took the wind out of his jaw. He de-escalated and responded with a lamb's gentleness, "Exactly." She kept her even-keeled firmness

131

and continued her teachable moment stating, "Why didn't you just say that...I can receive *that* as loving instead of what you just demonstrated."

In the situation above, my client was teaching her husband how to love her and treat her as an adult and life partner and not a subordinate to be reprimanded and beaten down. In the same way, loved ones oftentimes have to be educated on how best to love us as adults. This includes mothers who knew how to love their little ones with milk and cookies, clean and pretty dresses and kisses on "boo-boos," but may have no skills for loving adult daughters appropriately. As one of my girlfriends humorously declared, "My mother got me to the fourth grade and she was tapped out after that." The mother had nothing left to give in terms of her capacity to offer pearls of wisdom that would shepherd her daughter into womanhood and catapult her into lifelong personal growth. In fact, this was a common finding in my interviews with the subjects of this book. Most had mothers who were quite skilled at nurturing them as young offspring, but lost their way as the demands of parenting maturing minds called for greater finesse than was needed for the care of childish minds.

So, how do you teach an "old dog" (sorry for the crass comparison) new tricks? Glad you asked. As in the example with the husband and wife, you can always start by catching them right in the act of their misbehavior or miscommunication toward you and offer them a more productive alternative in approaching you right there *on the spot*. However, Mama may still not "get it" just from your instructive words alone, or she may think you're being picky or bossy or whatever. Hence, you will have your *best* chance for victory in this matter, in my observations, through *action*. So if Mom is demanding and thinks your time is her time, make yourself less available or delay your availability. Inform her that you'll get to her request at your earliest possible convenience—NOT necessarily at the moment she beckons. As the popular saying goes, "[her] lack of planning does not constitute an emergency for you." If you have the money-borrowing/squandering kind of mother, provide her with some educational tools for better money management. Additionally, make your wallet less available or *never* available for anything other than life-or-death situations, or limit the use of resources that you share with her to what YOU deem appropriate for her needs and/or some of her wants. If you have the "complaining/nothing's-ever-good-enough-and-you-should-have-done-better-by-me" kind of mom, expend far less energy, money and time providing gifts, taking her to upscale restaurants or planning trips with or for her. If she's the worrying type who wants you to check in with her by phone every time you cross the street, stop doing it and/or let voice mail pick up her calls. She will live.

The most important thing in how you reorient your mother toward a more adult relationship with you is that in any consequence you mete out, check your motive. If your motive is to just lash out, hurt and play tit for tat, STOP. Go back to the drawing board and pray for wisdom and guidance in how you establish boundaries with a pure heart. Your actions need to be guided by ultimate concern for the good of Mama's growth (which often requires tough love boundary-setting). OR your actions need to be guided by a dire need to protect and preserve your soul (so that you are more available for God and less available for Mama's tangled web).

3. Do Ask For Her Input Wherever Possible

Perhaps you've gotten in the habit of invalidating your mother's input and very likely for good reason. However, as a part of honoring her and making her feel needed (as everyone likes to feel), spend some time dwelling on your mother's positive attributes and those things you have in common. Pick benign areas of your life where you can ask for her input and find value in it. She'll probably light up like a firefly at the notion of being invited to offer her opinion. Perhaps it will satisfy her desire to intrude or volunteer her unsolicited opinion. This is the same tactic that celebrities use when they negotiate to *give* the media pictures of their big events in hopes of reduced intrusion by unwelcomed paparazzi. On the other hand, quite frankly, asking for your mother's input could backfire on you; you give her an inch and she could take a mile in terms of volunteering too much. Nevertheless, it's worth the experiment. Whatever the outcome, give her some kind of platform in your life such as: inviting her opinion on which dress you should wear to the party; asking her what to add to a new recipe to enhance flavoring; soliciting her opinion on the best way to save money or to pick the best meats or sweetest cantaloupes; or finding out her best strategy for keeping an orderly laundry room or removing stains. Soliciting her advice for something will likely go a long way toward making her feel valued. Even if it backfires, it's a small sacrifice on your part. Ask her SOMETHING and value it. Give her one small section of your garden in which to plant her seeds lest she burst at the seams. It will provide a bridge for peacemaking and an opportunity to catch her doing something right. Just as a farmer focuses his attention on nutrient-rich soil, planting seeds and watering for growing a good crop, so it is that what you decide to focus on in your relationship with your mother will likely grow.

4. Do Plug Into Life

One of the factors that may keep you stuck in bondage to your mother is limited choices concerning employment opportunities, companions, financial options, skills and trusted advisers. The more options you have to choose from, the less trapped you feel in a certain set of circumstances or in certain relational dynamics. Creating or increasing options begins with a self-assessment of your talents and skills, strengths and weaknesses. You may want to ask trusted friends or co-workers to help you identify your strengths, or you may begin to listen carefully to those aspects about yourself that people seem to notice or compliment. Try reconnecting with early interests and curiosities to rediscover your path in life, and look for a recurring pattern or theme. Once you have identified your most positive qualities, maximize them through educational advancement, vocational training, mentors and hobbies that encourage routine and purposeful connection to others and a sense of competency. The key word here is "routine" as opposed to "occasional." It is the *routine* of joining with others in shared activity that builds familiar, supportive community around you and an expanded network of people to rely upon. They will give you the "gift" of missing you when you're absent. These bonds not only help combat loneliness, passivity or inertia but also leads to a more satisfying and fulfilling life in general. The more interesting your life appears to others, the more valuable your input will be considered, which in turn enhances confidence in your thoughts and opinions. Furthermore, when you get plugged into life, you become too preoccupied with living your life to dwell on Mama's latest jabs or arrows.

Here's food for thought just as an aside: *Anyone* in your circle not willing to participate in respecting, supporting or even celebrating your desire to expand your horizons, including Mama, is not healthy for you. Unfortunately, some of these people will always be in your life if related to you by blood, and they may have to be loved from afar. Not everyone gets to sit in a front row seat to witness the unfolding masterpiece theater that is your life. Those seats are reserved for smiling and encouraging faces belonging to those who have demonstrated nothing but the best of intentions toward you even when they offered a word of caution, correction or critique.

5. Do Put Your Ears on Auditory Cruise Control

The Bible instructs us to guard our hearts, above all else, for the heart *is* the wellspring of life (Proverbs 4:23, emphasis added). One way to do this is by carefully screening what makes it past your ears and into your heart in the first place. If you have a mom who won't allow you to cut into or cut off her stream of compulsive complaints that define her conversation, and you feel drained at the end of a shared outing, then put your ears on auditory cruise control (ACC). By this, I encourage you to listen selectively as you filter out the white noise of tales of what somebody should have done and didn't, tales of what somebody didn't do and should have; harsh judgments of others' responses and choices; recounts of how people slighted her (though not detectable by others); criticisms of your dress being too short, or your dress being too long; comments about the grass being too green, the tree too tall, the red light too long, the billboard too distasteful and the sky too blue. In short, attune your ears to an airwave that translates and categorizes this cacophony into mere sounds similar to the monotonous "wha, wha, wha…wha, wha, wha" of Charlie Brown's teacher. You hear it, but you become numb to the drone of her complaints, which all sort of run together into an indistinguishable and distant sound such as the television in the background while you're washing dishes. You simply filter it out of your active thoughts and render it unworthy of response. You may relapse and get snagged here and there as the negativity breaks into your conscious awareness when Mama expresses something unbearably unkind, unjust or untrue. At those moments, you may find yourself increasingly irritable, agitated or "snagged" into inciting arguments out of your character. That happens, and that's okay. Remember, you're in the ring with Mike Tyson. Guard against getting hit with one of her left hooks because your jaw will indeed be shattered, and she'll be unflappably "ignorant" about how you managed to get hurt. So apologize if you become "slap-ugly" (as some of us say in the South) with your sinful retaliation. Own your unkindness, make repair to the best of your ability, reset your ACC and press on. Choose to respond selectively to constructive and more positive dialogue. In this way, you may be able to extinguish her fiery tongue for "without wood a fire goes out" (Proverbs 26:20). When you stop responding, her taste for bitter expressions, juicy gossip, salty dialogue or "sour grapes" may be lost.

OR you might try making your ACC even more powerful by combining this tool with *actions* that reflect you have heard the complaints and will not put her in a position to be so offended again. For example, a friend recently shared stories about her mother's inability to find anything or anybody faultless, in addition to her hypochondriac tendencies that often led to bogus trips to the doctor or hospital. She told me how her mother called her early one morning to make an emotionless declaration, without voicing much explanation or distress: "I need to go to the hospital." My friend, Joy, who was planning to attend a funeral of a close in-law that day, canceled her plans and made the trek to the hospital while suspecting that the entire ordeal was a ruse. Anyway, her mother's complaints of vague abdominal distress, after several tests were run, turned out to be......(drum roll please)......gas. My very patient friend Joy then treated her mother, Beatrice, to a scrumptious lunch at an upscale restaurant to appease her after the invasion of so many tests. You could probably guess that the lunch was polluted with the raw sewage of Beatrice's complaints about the meat being too rare, the salad dressing too sparse, the bread too lukewarm, the coffee too weak. Joy was able to turn on her ACC to get through the lunch without indigestion. In response to Joy's calmness and quiet resolve, Beatrice was more able to hear her own litany of complaints whirling around the table. Without resistance or engagement from Joy, she was forced to be "entertained" by her own monologue, which increased her self-awareness. One shocking thing happened at the end of the lunch: Beatrice had a rare moment of insight. She acknowledged her non-stop complaints. Joy, ever the peaceful one even as she saw her $42 lunch tab arrive, simply responded to her mother, "No problem. Next time, I'll just treat you to McDonald's." In other words, Joy was communicating to Mama, "Go ahead and complain on a much cheaper dime so that I won't have to cause you and my wallet to suffer through a 'miserable treat' of fine dining ever again." This is one way to let your actions, combined with ACC, do the talking.

In short, practice the art of either "checking out" or divesting your energy from the toxic deluge your mother may be capable of spewing your way. Put on a hazmat suit, clothing yourself in the full armor of God. Pray for her while she's complaining, or distract yourself during ACC with thoughts of what to cook for dinner, what you'll do when you get home, how you'll spend the evening, what you'll wear to work tomorrow, what you won't "subject" your mother to again such as an expensive lunch. Use any distraction available that will allow you to take your mind on a little mini-vacation.

6. Do Let Stuff Fall Through the Cracks on Purpose

If your mom is scheduling your time as though it is hers—to get her hair fixed, to take her to the doctor, to get her nails done, to shop for new curtains, to make returns to Target, to shop for new gadgets, to take the car for repairs, to pick out new carpet, to take her out to eat, to pick up her groceries, to make arrangements with a handyman to repair the garbage disposal—and you find it's all becoming a bit much, hit the pause button. Assuming she is still able to do things for herself and is in her right mind, provide her with a master list of resources for help. Keep directing her back to that list when she calls you for help. Be available for the first few repair visits and then implement the "I-think-you-can-do-this-and-let-me-show-you-how" program. You can then promote her to the "you're-pretty-much-on-your-own" program, which will help her to grow in confidence and self-sufficiency. Additionally, you may need to allow certain things to become uncomfortably dysfunctional in her life. In so doing, she will be compelled to act more independently and decisively in the same way a toddler eventually becomes uncomfortable with soiled diapers enough to become proactive in toilet training. It's how we grow—out of our discomforts and pains.

As my own widowed mother aged and began to waste energy and money on endless repairs of her forty-two-year-old home, which had become a money pit rivaling the house in the movie by that same name, I started my campaign for her to come live with us. She wasn't hearing it AT ALL—that is, as long as *I* was running around helping her keep the house intact—making phone calls, researching handymen, doing the legwork to find proper materials and comparing vinyl floor samples. When I made the conscious decision to stop rowing the boat to keep her house afloat and refused to shop for one more linoleum floor or one more set of curtains or one more *anything*, she soon developed 20/20 vision and was able to *see* more clearly the need to let the house go and move on. With my intentional passive resistance, I helped her reach the conclusion that she could not take care of that house and neither could I without neglecting my own household. She moved in with us a couple of years later. The fact that she is with us is no less a miracle than the parting of the Red Sea, but that "miracle" would never have happened without me setting a much-needed boundary.

7. Do Use the "I Think, However, So…Formula"

Robert Danielle, PhD, taught me this assertiveness formula during graduate school training, and I have altered it a bit over the years. It is similar to the sandwich technique used in management circles wherein you sandwich your expression of a problem in between two positive statements. I have taught it to many others and find it to be the most useful tool for respectfully getting your needs met by others *most of the time*. When you want to confront a potential disagreement with Mama productively, start off with an honest compliment. This sometimes requires creative thinking if she's usually the antagonist in the ever-thickening plot of your relationship drama. Keep in mind that an individual's strongest attributes are often the same characteristics that get under another's skin when use of these characteristics is unrestrained (e.g., the one with a great eye for detail who ends up being a thorn in everybody's flesh because her perfectionism impractically delays projects by trying to meet unreasonable standards). Also, keep in mind that everybody has at least one redeeming quality. Search for it in your mother and always begin a prickly discussion with sincere appreciation for a unique trait that's somehow related to the topic at hand. This usually prepares the way for constructive dialogue because positive feedback is uncommon, particularly when it is directed at a family member who may often be taken for granted. Hence, it gets attention and opens ears. People are usually smart enough to detect phony compliments for the purpose of manipulation, so express honesty above all else.

For starters, examples may include, "*I* **think** you work really hard," "*I* **appreciate** your thoughtfulness," "*I* **admire** your desire to help with the kids." Next, move into the explanation of your problem starting off with "I" language *only* such as "**however** *I* am feeling challenged with…**however** *I* am having a problem with…**however** *I* am experiencing…**however** *I* am confused about…." Using "I" language makes it seem as though the problem *is* really yours, and most reasonable people want to help you with *your* problem. Hence it is most important to avoid explaining your problem by beginning with the word "you," which may make the listener feel attacked. This raises defenses and closes ears to what you have to say. Also be careful to use "however" instead of "but" because the word "but" tends to nullify all the positives that came before it. Lastly, the "**so**" part of the formula is a statement of the solution to the problem that has some benefit (not perfect answers) for each of you. From the outset you must spend time thinking about the desired outcome and present it with politeness and firmness in a way that gives consideration to Mama *and* yourself. This is where you, the "savvy salesman," close the deal with phrasing like, "**So** my suggestion is…**so** I have prepared a schedule…**so** I'm thinking we both can benefit if…." When you confront someone about a potential conflict, problem or disagreement, your entire position is weakened if you don't have a thoughtful solution to propose. Giving forethought to problem resolution produces clarity, without unproductive emotional venting, that Mama may be able to digest and support.

8. Do Honor Her

Even if you've never stepped foot in a church or synagogue or ever read the Bible, no doubt you have heard somewhere that one of the Ten Commandments says something about honoring your mother. It is actually the sixth commandment, and it reads: "Honor your father and your mother, as the Lord your God has commanded you, so that you may live long and that it may go well with you in the land the Lord your God is giving you." (Deuteronomy 5:16). Hmmm. That last phrase is worth a pause: "*so that* you may live long and that it may go well with you…" (emphasis added). According to this scripture, there is a big incentive to honor your parents, one of which may be an opportunity to live a long life, and the other appears to be some kind of blessing that is not made explicit in this passage. Though I can't begin to tell you all that God had in mind when He wrote this in stone, I do know it behooves us to take heed to that which God commands. Notice, there weren't any conditions attached to it as in "honor her if she was the best mom in the world" or "honor her if she's never hurt you" or "honor her if she's pleasant to be around."

Also, consider the teaching of Proverbs 1:8-9, "…and do not forsake your mother's teaching. [It will be] a garland to grace your head and a chain to adorn your neck." Key words for me here are *grace* and *adorn* because these speak of embellishments that distinguish, bring attention to or enhance appearance in ways that catch the eyes and potentially draw others unto the wearer. Hence, the teachings from Mom, though they may come at a price, are ultimately designed to enhance and distinguish you *while* serving as constant, obvious and visible reminders of your journey and triumphs. The teachings become adornments in the same way the adornment of a diamond necklace given from husband to wife for an anniversary gift might remind the couple of shared milestones and bittersweet struggles together. Both the sixth commandment and Proverbs 1:8-9 indicate definite benefit to the one who honors Mama and remembers her teaching.

To expound further, I think we can all agree that, regardless of her parenting style or intentions, your mother did two undeniable things that distinguish you: 1) She served as the vessel that brought your one-of-a-kind being into this world and endured all the physical sacrifices that entails; and 2) She provided you the opportunity to learn many unique lessons through her— sometimes *because of* her and sometimes *in spite of* her.

Mama's Priceless Lessons for the Road Ahead

If you had the kind of mother who passed along life lessons in words or deeds, and her wisdom reverberates in your life today, it's a no-brainer to realize the positive impact of her teaching on your life. If you had the kind of mother who wasn't able—for whatever reason—to teach you much (so you thought), and perhaps she even worked against your growth and exposure, the positive lessons she taught may be more difficult to discern. However, don't get it confused; she still taught you much—if you allow it, however hard earned the lesson was to receive. These sometimes tarnished lessons from the school of hard knocks need to be polished, just as dross must be removed from fine silver in order to appreciate its beauty. These lessons are not to be overlooked, but should rather be seen as enhancement for the way in which you are "graced" or "adorned" before others. In other words, there is much for you and others to gain from allowing the good, bad and ugly of your mother's examples to work *for you* and *not against you* (which may require intensive therapy for some of you).

Therefore, her inaccessibility or limited wisdom may have *taught* you to find answers for yourself when others couldn't or can't provide them. The emotional turmoil she created in your life may have *taught* you to transcend circumstances or to make friends more easily because you *had to* in order to survive. The type of marriage or relationships she courted may have *taught* you what dysfunctional relationships look like and the importance of guarding against them. Her complaining tongue and ungrateful heart may have *taught* you how to love the unlovable. Her mental illness and chronic vulnerability may have *taught* you patience and compassion for those who can't do for themselves. Her underachievement or under-exposure may have *taught* you to strive for the moon. Her discouragement may have *taught* you to persevere in overcoming naysayers and detractors as you were passionately motivated to prove them wrong. Her overbearing nature may have *taught* you to stand on your own convictions with resolve in the face of opposition. Her jealous, manipulative or downright abusive ways may have *taught* you how to recognize those who mean you no good and how to distance and protect yourself accordingly. Her critical attacks against you may have *taught* you to savor joyful moments and to carefully select relationships that support and edify you. Her parenting deficiencies may have *taught* you to be a more loving, thoughtful and engaged mother. Most importantly, her emotional, educational, financial or physical deficits that negatively impacted your life may have taught you to hunger and thirst for a rescuer, a protector, a provider, a savior in the person of Jesus Christ.

God promises in Psalm 27:10 (KJV), "When [your] father and [your] mother forsake [you], then the Lord will take [you] up". As a result, the gloriously rich and abounding harvest produced in you and in those influenced by you, from all the "wisdom" of your mother's teachings, intentional or accidental, will indeed honor her.

Somebody ought to shout AMEN!

References

Bible (New International Version).

Bible (King James Version).

About the Author

NATIVE ATLANTAN Dr. Pamela Everett Thompson, a clinical psychologist and professional life coach, has interviewed thousands of women and adolescent females over the course of fifteen years in the field of mental health. She has owned and operated her private practice in Atlanta since 2004 and has provided clinical services for prisons and group homes throughout the state of Georgia since 2002. It is her passion to make the idea of getting help from a psychologist user-friendly and accessible in various settings. Thus she added community forums, seminars, writing and life-coaching components to her practice in 2007. This has allowed her to be a positive influence well beyond the four walls of her practice or the confines of Atlanta in order to take psychology "to the streets," debunking the myth that it's just for "crazy people." All of her varied professional experiences have exposed her to women's issues in particular, across the lifespan, where an intense focus on "Mama" often enters the equation. Hence, she has been inspired by throngs of women who have courageously shared their stories, concerning strained relationships of all kinds, to begin putting her trained observations into writing. It is her desire to use her writing as a tool of self-discovery, healing and transformation.

Dr. Thompson's first career in public relations has afforded her a unique comfort level in her communication skills that nudges interviewees to confront the "elephant in the room" head-on. She is best known for integrating her clinical skills and knowledge with a biblical worldview, though she has been delighted to provide services for people of all faiths. However, her greatest joy in her professional life is derived from serving those who desire help in applying biblical instruction and clinical guidance in decision-making, problem-solving, relationship attraction and maintenance and daily life in general. She is available for life coaching, workshops and seminars and may be contacted through www.drpamthompson.com.

CPSIA information can be obtained
at www.ICGtesting.com
Printed in the USA
FFOW01n0735200214
3670FF